Sara Thurman

Reflecting on Pain and Moving Beyond Grief:

Living With Loss and Discovering
New Meaning

The artwork on the cover of this book is a painting that I completed on the 98th day after losing my husband, Wayman. I titled the work, *Beside Peaceful Streams*. I had gone that day to sit by a beautiful creek in the Texas Hill Country. I placed a single, yellow wildflower in the creek and watched it slowly drift away from me.

I started this painting with all reds and then an orange layer. Next, I added layers of blues. I added a yellow flower in the lower left corner which moved along the upper right corner and edge, and eventually out of sight, symbolic of Wayman leaving. This painting hangs in my guest room and reminds me of my journey and the peaceful streams God has given me to sit by for restoration and healing.

My poem, Beside Peaceful Streams, was completed upon my return home as I expressed the sorrow of releasing "My Man." I had felt God's peace by the water and heard his voice in this poem.

Since Wayman passed, writing poetry and prose has been therapeutic. There is something about putting words together that helps my pain. Giving language to my pain and sorrow, grief and loneliness has been healing. I find I want my words to have rhythm and meaning in order to capture all that we had. It helps me take the next step. To take the next breath.

> *You are not alone. Jesus is with you. Always.*

Beside Peaceful Streams

By Sara Thurman

My heart breaks into a thousand pieces as
I search for the peaceful streams.

You are the one to lead me beside peaceful streams.

Jesus answered me,

"Receive My rest and renewed strength for your soul as you continue
your journey beside peaceful streams."

ISBN Paperback: 978-1-7341560-8-9
ISBN Electronic: 978-1-7341560-9-6
Library of Congress Control Number: 2021921411

Printed in the United States of America.

Acts 1:8 Blessings
Sara@SaraThurman.com
www.SaraThurman.com

All emphasis within Scripture quotations is the author's own. Certain pronouns in Scripture that refer to the Father, Son, Holy Spirit are capitalized and may differ from some publishers' styles.

Details in some anecdotes and stories have been changed to protect the identities of the persons involved. Details have been recalled to the best of the author's memory.

Dedication

I dedicate this book to my dearest forever friend, Ann Younger.

Ann, you taught me to see only the best in others,
and in myself when my eyes were tear stained.

You taught me to listen to the still, quiet voice of my
Jesus when my heart needed truth to win over the lies.

You taught me that the essence of true friendship is kindness,
acceptance, vulnerability, tears, and really good belly laughs.

You taught me to taste and see that the Lord is good—all the time.

You taught me to enjoy every moment of every
day—for it may be our last.

You taught me to live in the presence of Jesus through the hardest days
of my life—after My Man left this earth.

Because of you guiding me through my pain to places of healing
during my grief journey, this book is my story.

You taught me to love the one in front of me with all my being because
Jesus showed us how.

Ann Younger, I am thankful for you, my forever friend!

I am so blessed to have eternity to create with you.

Join my email list at https://sarathurman.com to follow my grief support groups, online and in-person creative spiritual retreats, virtual trainings, and upcoming books. You may also purchase my books, artwork, and more on this website. I also offer creative spiritual retreats and classes, some specifically on loss and grieving. I am a Certified Grief Educator, having completed a program led by grief expert David Kessler. Contact me for my latest offerings.

Table Of Contents

Foreword

During my thirty years as a psychotherapist, I have read many books about grieving. This is the most intimate portrait of grief I have encountered. With searing honesty, Sara recounts her first 100 days of grief after her beloved husband, Wayman's, death. It is sometimes hard to read. Her faith and deeply personal walk with God shines through each entry. Her faith is her anchor in the most difficult of times, even as she questions taking her own life.

Sara has done intensive study with David Kessler, an iconic figure in the field of grief counseling. As a result, her counsel is trustworthy and professionally sound.

As a therapist, I appreciate her guidance for well-meaning people on what NOT to say to those in grief and what NOT to do in an effort to help.

In addition to being a psychotherapist, I am a mother who lost a beloved daughter to early death. Sara's heart rendering entries of groaning in a grief that is beyond words spoke to a place I know intimately.

May Sara's deeply honest story of her grief journey enable and inspire you to fully live your own journey. May peace be with you.

Judy Bennett, M.A., LPC

Wimberley, Texas

Preface

I have been a journalist since I was a teenager, so closing in on fifty years now. Writing my thoughts, my prayers, scripture, and what I hear Jesus telling me is a nearly daily habit. Now I see the value of my written words penned alongside my own grief journey.

This book was birthed from my personal journal in which I documented my grief journey. "Document the journey" is advice I often give to others. Documenting the journey gives you a written record of where you have been and what you have overcome. More importantly, it allows your heart to speak personally with God and provides a place to express your fears, loves, hurts, joys, etc. in a one-on-one conversation with God. A place where you can ask Him questions, write His answers, meditate on scriptures, and reference when you need reminders of His love and promise of eternal life.

This book is not meant to replace professional help for someone who is contemplating taking their life. If you are in such a place of darkness in your grief, where death seems to be the only answer, please reach out for help from a professional counselor or a trusted friend or family member. Help is waiting for you, to pull you back to Light.

Why did I write my private journey for all to see? The answer is multifold. One reason was for me. By writing this prayer journal, my healing and grief became clearer, and more bearable, because of the deep processing of emotions required to write my journey.

The second reason was for you. For you to have a guide to process your own grief, unique to your situation and story. Your own story of grief is so important and needs to be witnessed by others in order for you to heal and make progress while on your winding road of grief.

The third reason is Jesus. I pray my story will help you see the goodness of God inside *your* story. There is so much we do not understand about God's timing. His mysteries about death, and so much more, are veiled realities. But Jesus is the answer to every question. Some answers we will not know until we are on the other side of this physical life, but, in the meantime, we can ask and cry and seek His face and comfort. And those of us in grief keep going, day by day, to see the sunrise and the sunset, asking for strength to make it to another day.

And another reason I wrote this book is because of the value of God's written Word; His Bible to bring comfort through scripture, pouring healing oil into our broken, bleeding souls. My original intent was to include only twenty or thirty scriptures in this prayer journal book. But God had other plans. Once I counted and read all the scriptures I had noted in the first 100 days of my grief journey, I realized I had more than sixty references to God's Holy Word. How could I not include His words that brought me comfort and direction, purpose and life, and **strength** in the midst of my first 100 days of grief? I am thankful God was there for me in His Word, pouring His oil into the wounds of my broken heart.

An option for you to include in your journey is my scripture cards with my unique original paintings on one side and the anchor verses God specifically gave to me during my first 100 days of grieving for my husband. I pray they bless you with comfort and hope.

My beloved husband of nearly thirty-five years, "My Man," Wayman Lee Thurman, was called home to Jesus on January 19, 2020.

The first 100 days after his passing were brutal, and so very difficult. I shared openly my tears and groans with my followers on social media. Many wrote to me to say:

"Thanks, Sara. You are helping me grieve my loss from five years ago. You are showing us how to grieve in a different way. To just be "in the grief." And to not push it away. To sit in the midst of my grief."

My practice of journaling was a gift to my heart as I read about my broken and bleeding heart. I wrote the words. The scriptures. The cries. The groans. The reality of my grief. I knew my own grief journey was not over when I finished writing this book. It doesn't "end" after 100 days, a year, five years, etc. My grief will end, and my joy will be complete when I see Jesus and Wayman, face to face.

"A deep sorrow, especially caused by someone's death," is Google's definition of grief. Grief is such an individual process, unique to our love, our personalities, our relationships. Our own grief stories. There is no wrong way to grieve. There is no right way to grieve. There is just grief. Oh, such a deep sorrow, this thing called grief.

I believe this book is for grieving widows, since that is my perspective. But I also believe we all go through grief differently, and my prayer is that this book can be a resource for anyone going through loss, even divorce. Dreams unrealized are also reasons to grieve. The loss of a child, parent, sibling, and friend all are unique pathways of grief we may travel in this life. During this time of grief, scriptures can show you God's plans for you and remind you how to give your grief and sorrow to Him to help you carry the burden. Use the scriptures in this book as your anchors during grief. Scriptures are anchors for all of us.

My prayer is also that this book can be a help to others who are walking with loved ones in deep grief. Use your own special journal or my Companion Reflection Journal to express your own thoughts, prayers, scriptures, and responses to the journal prompts for each day. I love leather journals, but there are many journal choices. Pick what appeals to you. Even a yellow legal pad works. Make it yours.

I am privileged to be walking this journey with you. Let this book be a guide, but know that God is your true guide, holding you so very close to His heart. I know God is with you in unique and precious ways. May God come and sit with you as He has never before.

Jesus's words from Matthew 5:4 NLT were my anchor scripture for this book.

"God blesses those who mourn, for they will be comforted."

It is my prayer for you to know the deep, deep comfort of God in the midst of your grief journey, from day one until you see the beautiful face of Jesus. May you feel God's never-ending love and experience the goodness of God on this side of heaven in your journey of grief.

Introduction

My life was forever changed on January 19, 2020, when My Man passed from this earth. Wayman Lee Thurman was the strong, wise, and gentle wind beneath my wings who was my voice of love. We celebrated an epic love story for thirty-five years.

I had never considered writing a book about grief. It was not in my plans at all. But I believe God had a different plan. As I lived the first 100 days without My Man, I never knew anything could be so hard. Our culture has not mastered the art of grieving well.

I know that my grief journey is not over. I am not in the middle of my grief journey. I'm just at the tiny little edge of the beginnings of my grief journey. So why would I begin this book specifically about the first 100 days of my grief journey? I was given an assignment from God to share my journey, to share my journal and thoughts and pain.

Through sharing the first months of my grief on Facebook and other social media outlets, I knew God had assigned me the task of sharing my story in written form. On day seventy-nine, I felt in my spirit God telling me to write this book about my first 100 days of grief. Of course, my grief journey has been, and will be, long, hard, and arduous with many twists and turns. But for this part of my journey, it will tell the story of my first 100 days, with some additional afterward stories. Then, on day eighty-nine, God said to me, "Make it a journal. Give my people a place to write their own story." Oh, I love it when God is right in the middle of my thoughts!

My prayer is that this book will bring hope and healing to all those who read it. And that all who read this book will know a little more about how to navigate their grief journey and the grief journey of those they love. I pray my book can bring forth some meaning to others in need. Nothing is harder on this side of heaven than to lose a loved one.

Eternity is something I have been asking God for understanding of. I know My Man has eternity already. And I believe I have eternity as well. But for a slice of time, we are not on the same side of the line. So, I wait, with great expectation for the reunion with My Man. And then I will understand the greatest gift of all, living for all eternity with My Man and God.

I will share my unique path of grief (it won't be like yours), my journey, my thoughts, my seasons within the first 100 days after Wayman passed from this earthly life into eternity. As I began writing this book, I soon understood I also needed to include what my life has been like beyond the first 100 days. Therefore, I will share more details of my transitions and how I have found meaning in my life while integrating the pain and grief from losing My Man. I have learned to live past the reality of the death of My Man. And I want you to learn how to live again, too.

I can't remember very much about some of those days. My brain was numb. I didn't realize at the time how much I was not able to do normal life. I could only do so much every day. It was so hard to just get out of bed. To breathe. To eat. To take a walk. To sleep. To cry. And then cry some more. To groan deeply in my loss. I didn't even know my body was capable of such deep groans of pain. I had never felt such loneliness and pain. Ever.

> *Feel the feelings. If you do, you can heal.*

The Banana Story

Today I took my granddaughter, Hepzibah Spring Thurman, to the park with an unpeeled banana and her water bottle. She peeled her banana, broke it in half, held it in her two hands, and ate it as we walked along the winding sidewalk on our way to the slides and swings.

As I think about this day I cry and know God is so much more than I can comprehend. But I receive glimpses of His eternal love. See, about 457 days ago this little grand was only nine months old and did not like bananas. But on the morning of her Papa's last day on earth he saw her in a vision, with a banana in each hand. He started talking to her with such excitement, it was as though she was in the ICU room. He saw into the unseen that day. But she was far on the other side of the world. I am so thankful I was there in the room to witness this conversation with his granddaughter.

Today, this precious little girl loves bananas. Just like her Papa saw from his hospital bed on January 19, 2020. I believe her Papa is still watching her every step from the balconies of heaven. He is so very happy she loves bananas as they were an essential daily fruit for him.

Will you praise God believing the unseen realm is eternal? God is revealing to His children more and more of Himself as we focus our attention on the unseen.

2 Corinthians 4:18 TPT

*"...because we don't focus our attention on what is seen
but on what is unseen. For what is seen is temporary,
but the unseen realm is eternal."*

Written April 21, 2021

*"God blesses those who mourn, for they
will be comforted."*

Matthew 5:4 NLT

Our Epic Love Story

To really understand my story of grief, I want you to know about My Man and our love story. Our relationship was so special and had unique and beautiful threads of love running right down the middle.

Wayman was a good friend of my parents before we started dating. They spent time together on weekends, went to church together, and enjoyed each other's company. In the spring of 1985, Wayman asked my parents to attend a symphony concert in San Angelo, Texas. He mentioned to my father it would be nice if I would join them. So, my father called and asked me to go. I adamantly said, "If Wayman wants me to come, he needs to call me himself and ask me." And in just a few days, Wayman called to invite me to the symphony and also to the private reception afterwards for the guest violinist. I accepted the invitation and was excited in my heart for a date with this man. It ended up that I had to drive three hours through an unexpected snow and ice storm to get to this first date with My Man. It was so worth the drive!

So, a little background information will help you understand our story even more. I was twenty-six years old and had recently told God, a few months before I started dating Wayman, that I was ok to be an "old-maid schoolteacher." I told God I wanted the best husband possible, and I was willing to wait a long time. And I was ok being single if He could not give me the best husband possible. Upon reflection, I realized when I ask God for something, I believe He will answer. God answered "big" on our first date.

My parents attended the symphony concert as well. Afterwards Wayman and I went to the private reception and then went country and western dancing (a thing in Texas). On this first date, I asked Wayman how old he was. He had never told my parents. I did not even blink an eye when he told me, "Forty-seven years old." Wayman was twenty years older than me. This reality was a huge surprise, but it did not keep me from falling in love with him that night. That Saturday night in

3

February 1985, I knew in my heart this man would be my husband. We were married three months later on May 19, 1985, in an outside wedding near the Concho River in San Angelo, Texas.

I have a belief that husbands and wives should help each other be the best they can be. Marriage should bring out the best in each partner so each person can become way more than they could ever be on their own. I knew every second of every minute in all of our years together that Wayman Lee Thurman was the best husband and that God had picked him for *me*, to be my partner. I became a much better person because of marrying Wayman.

We had some rough times in our marriage. For example, we struggled to get pregnant for the first five years of our marriage. This situation caused much angst between us. Then, after five years of trying to get pregnant, God gave us a son together, and then twenty months later, another son.

We had financial crises. We were unemployed for a season and lost everything in the physical realm of money. We declared bankruptcy and had to start over in humility. God was with us. These trials in our marriage only drew us together more. We endured the hard times to get to the place of peace and joy with simple uncomplicated lives.

Wayman and I had so many similar interests. We loved being in nature, taking walks, camping, snow skiing, traveling to new places, and sharing our simple home and meals together. We were best friends. We did not have secrets. We served each other with a deep love. We laughed together. We cried together. We prayed together. We loved life together. We taught and parented two incredible sons together. We dreamed together. We were peaceful together. We were a holy communion. Wayman's love ran so deep and wide, high and low. Therefore, his passing left a deep rugged crevasse in my heart.

> *Today is not the end. It is only the beginning.*

The Picture

By Sara Thurman

We sit side by side as close as possible in our backyard sanctuary on the bench you made. You have a grin on your face portraying a deep, wide, and long and high love for me. I am smiling from ear to ear, feeling safe and loved. I can tell your smile is a message right to my heart. I am thankful for this picture of our love. It ministers to a deep place in my soul.

This photograph was displayed at your service, a statement of our love to everyone who entered. 24 x 36 can't be missed. In the few weeks I was home after you passed, I had the picture hanging in my bedroom, our bedroom. I cried every time I looked at it. And in those days, I was crying most of the time.

Then I went away for a few months. It was COVID time. It was so lonely at home, and I needed more support. I couldn't be home without you. I went to live with Justin and Ana and Lilian for a few months. Then I went to live with Ann and Roland for a month. And then I got brave and knew it was time to come home.

When I came home, I knew I could not have the picture of us in my bedroom. It was too sad. It was too hard. So, the picture went under the bed in the guest bedroom. I knew I could not see it every day. It was too big. My heart was bleeding. When I saw it the pain of missing you was too much. So, I hid us.

And then, a few weeks before you had been gone a year, I pulled us out from under the guest bed. I dusted us off and put us on the fireplace hearth in the living room. For the first few weeks I sat on the couch or in your chair and looked at us. I cried. And I cried. Every time I looked at us, I cried. I remembered the gift of our marriage. And the life we had together. And I cried.

I wondered how long I would leave the picture of us on the fireplace hearth. Would I hide us under the bed again? Would the pain continue to be so great that I could not breathe? Would I lay on the floor and moan and weep until I ran out of tears?

I was not in a rush to put us away. In fact, we are still there. On the fireplace hearth. Going on five months, we are still there. Smiling and hugging. Peaceful and full of joy. Reminding me of your great love for me. I can look at this picture and know deep in my heart how much you loved me. I think you might have even been pinching my bottom for fun in the midst of this photo shoot in January 2019. With every ounce of who you were, you loved me. You loved me so well. I can see it on your face. In your smile. With your hand around me, holding me close. I am so thankful to remember your deep love for me. I can say, "Wayman really loved me."

So, for now, the picture of us is still on display as a symbol of our love. When guests arrive, it is a focal point in my (or do I say "our") living room. Oh, this transition of being a widow is not easy. How long will I leave us on the hearth? I really don't know. But for now, we are there. My heart is not bleeding so much. I can look at us and smile. And be thankful for us. So very thankful to have known a love like yours. Unconditional and everlasting. Thank you, Wayman.

Mother's Day, May 9, 2021

My Anchor and Plumb Line for the First 100 Days

Scriptures and Prayers I Wrote in My Journal in the First 100 Days After Losing Wayman

As I stated earlier, I have been journaling for many years. It is something I started long before losing Wayman. When I journal, it has always been an open conversation between me and God. I write scripture that speaks to me, my desires, hurts, fears, gratitude, prayers, etc., and God responds to me through what I call my "Jesus Stream." I write His responses below each journal entry. On the corresponding days I asked God for a journal prompt for you. You can choose to use my prompt or be prompted by the Holy Spirit and your own conversations with God.

I will now share with you my journal entries and my Jesus Streams.

Ten days before Wayman passed. (We had no indication he was ten days from dying.) These are the words God shared with me that day.

Jesus Stream, January 9, 2020.

Have no fear. God is with you, Sara Lee. Here we go. I am with you. Praise Me. All eyes on Me. You are My delight. I love you.

Psalm 46:4 NLT
"A river brings joy to the city of our God."

The sacred home of the Most High. So daughter, My JOY is yours. Today. Enjoy this day. Envelope yourself in Me. So be the river of joy. I love you. Rest in Me for every single thing you need. So, rest in Me. Have fun. Yes, and amen, dear one. I have this. Be My river. Jump into My river. Connect with My joy! Have fun! Be blessed, dear one.

Journal Prompt

How would you describe your walk with God before your loss? Do you have any promises from God's heart to yours that you can lean on during this time? Ask God for more promises.

Some days I wrote nothing in my journal. Grief held me in silence and shock. I could not write in my numbness. I was barely breathing. If you desire to fill in the blanks as Jesus leads you, I am leaving space for you to write on each of the 100 days. But please know, if the pain is too great, it is ok not to write on some days.

Accept My Rest

By Sara Thurman

When you feel the pull of perfectionism, accept My rest.

Accept My rest even if it feels like swimming upstream,
not wanting to stop.

Oh, Beautiful One, accept My rest as I lead
our dance together into eternity.

October 20, 2020

Overview of
My First 25 Days

Feelings: I was numb. I was in shock. I did not know what to do or what to say. My Man was gone. I was deeply sad, sadder than I had ever been in my life. Some days I was unable to write anything. My pain was overwhelming, and I was unable to access the part of me that could write. Going forward, you will see some dates with no entry. These are the days my grief paralyzed me. I could not write. I have marked these days in this book with, "Selah, quiet interlude" to identify them.

What I needed most:

- Empathetic hearts and listening ears to witness my brokenness.

- Someone who had the time to listen if they asked me how I was doing.

- Someone to bring me a few healthy meals I could easily prepare and then freeze the leftovers.

- Someone to go on a walk with me. Or to go to a park to sit and talk. I needed to be outside.

- I was unable to make decisions, so I needed to be given two choices for which I could answer yes or no.

- I needed to take one hour at a time. One day at a time. I could not think about tomorrow. It was too painful.

- I needed extra companionship and times to look forward to with friends.

- I needed to feel the pain of each hour. Tears are beautiful and are needed to cleanse the body.

- I needed to cry. Cry. Cry. Let the tears flow.

What I did not need:

🌱 Being told I would get better. I wanted to feel the pain of my loss. Do not discount my pain by telling me "Time will heal."

🌱 To be told my loved one was in a better place. The pain is so deep; I needed to come to this realization myself in my own time.

Transitions I noticed during this time:

🌱 Hope is beginning to rise over despair in parts of some days.

Day 1, January 19, 2020, Selah, quiet interlude

Day 2, January 20, 2020, Selah, quiet interlude

> *I know you are tired of being so sad. But be sad today because at some point 'tomorrow' you won't be as sad as you are today.*

Day 3, January 21, 2020, Selah, quiet interlude

Day 4, January 22, 2020, Selah, quiet interlude

Day 5, January 23, 2020, Selah, quiet interlude

Day 6, January 24, 2020, Selah, quiet interlude

Day 7, January 25, 2020, Selah, quiet interlude

Day 8, January 26, 2020, Selah, quiet interlude

Journal Prompt

My strongest emotions during these days were intense sadness and loneliness. What was your strongest emotion in the first few days after your loss? What did you tell yourself about that emotion? How did you share that emotion with God and how did He answer?

Day 9, January 27, 2020

(First journal entry after Wayman left this earth.)

Dear Jesus, oh, how my heart aches. Could we push back time? Could we have a redo? But You God are holding me. I am hiding in the folds of Your robe. You are breathing strength on me. I am buying new bird seed.

Jesus Stream

Oh, My beautiful one. I am right here. So so close. Even in your breaths and sobs and groans and tears and yells and silence. I am here. Look for Me, even in My outer garments. I will hide you there. You can weep and cry and be as loud as you need to be. Or as silent. You cannot get this wrong. I know your heart is breaking and bleeding and gushing open to where you think you will not make it.

Journal Prompt

Embrace the truth of grieving how *you* need to grieve. You cannot get this wrong. You have the freedom to grieve uniquely. What does freedom in your grief feel like in this time of loss? Can you find Jesus?

Day 10, January 28, 2020

Jesus, this is hard. It is so very hard. Help me. Guide me. Hold me. Cry with me. I am so sad. But I have peace that My Man is with you. Safe and sound and saved. Oh, Jesus.

Psalm 34:18 TPT

"The Lord is close to all whose hearts are crushed by pain."

My pain of not reaching out for My Man. For not soothing his hair. Never cutting his hair again. Snuggling. Never to bring him a cup of green tea again. Oh, Lord. Today - hold me. Hide me. Make the way, oh, Jesus. Thanks so much.

Journal Prompt

What do you miss the most about the person you are grieving? Let God know. Are you experiencing God's closeness as your heart is crushed by pain? If so, tell Him.

Day 11, January 29, 2020, Selah, quiet interlude

Day 12, January 30, 2020, Selah, quiet interlude

Journal Prompt

Do you have days you are unable to write? If so, what do you do those days and how do you connect with and feel close to God on those days? Does being outside and feeling the wind on your face, the sun on your skin, or tasting the rain, or maybe the smell of autumn leaves, bring you closer to Him?

Day 13, January 31, 2020

Oh, Jesus — Can I do this? This life without My Man? Oh, Jesus. This is hard. I can hear Wayman telling me, "Of course you can!" Oh, My Man. Thanks for pouring into me. For loving me with such fierceness that I knew without a doubt I was loved. A confidence that I am loved by God. I never doubted your love, Wayman Lee Thurman. I am grateful. Thankful. Blessed. Transformed by your love. You got this love from Jesus. And poured it into my heart. On Jordan and Justin. Thank You, Jesus. Keep pouring. Keep pouring on my heart. So, thank You, Jesus.

> *If you need help, ask for help.*

Jesus Stream

I am with you. Every second. Every minute. Every hour. Every day. Every month. Every year. Do you see how I am holding you? You are mine. You are not alone. It may feel like you are alone—but the truth is I have gone before you. I have taken care of everything. Watch Me. Trust Me. Hold onto Me. Lift your eyes. I am God Almighty. I am the I AM. I am holding you tightly. Breathe Me in. Do not think about tomorrow. Today is enough. Praise to the King. I love you, dear one. I am using you to bring light into the darkness. All glory to Me. Keep on praising Me. I love you, Sara! Love, Jesus.

Journal Prompt

Write to Jesus and tell Him about the present reality of the pain of this day. Can you hear any instruction from Jesus? Can you trust Him today? What is the hardest part? Tell Him.

Day 14, February 1, 2020

I am in such pain. So much grief from My Man being gone. Thirteen days. O Lord God, it is so hard. Time. Sleep. Food. Everything is different now. Every single thing is different. Lord help me find a rhythm of You. In my pain, will You surround me with Your angels? Lord, my pain is great. But I can tell when I praise You, all of heaven joins in. Oh February, you are so hard to embrace. To love deeply, one must grieve deeply.

Psalm 89:5 NLT

"All heaven will praise your great wonders, Lord: myriads of angels will praise you for your faithfulness."

Jesus Stream

Oh, my dear Sara — you are not alone. I have you surrounded. I have you, providing everything you need. I am with you dear one. I will make everything OK. We have this. Every second of every day. Watch Me. Hear from Me. Learn from Me. Trust Me. The veil is thin now. Listen to My voice. I will give you new revelations. New wisdom. New books. New art. So just rest in Me. I am with you, dear one. I am crying with you.

> Laugh out loud. You will feel better.

Journal Prompt

Can you tell God how difficult this journey is? Is anything the same? Tell Him. Are you feeling any shift if you praise God in any manner? Share. Do you know the angels are praising God with you? You are not alone.

Day 15, February 2, 2020

Oh, Wayman — I miss you. Today is two weeks. But God. I use this phrase often. But God. God is the God of the impossible. Many times, in my life God was the answer to what was and is still unknown. This quote from Corrie ten Boom always blesses me.

"Never be afraid to trust an unknown future to a known God."

Isaiah 55:8-9 TPT

"For My thoughts about mercy are not like your thoughts, and My ways are different from yours. As high as the heavens are above the earth, so My ways and My thoughts are higher than yours."

Jesus Stream

Oh, My daughter, trust Me. I know it all. I can see beyond this physical life. My love for Wayman is so great, I took him home. It was My plan all along. My mercy is abundant and generous. Trust Me. And yes, but Me. I will help you with your thoughts. It is a process that takes time. Let Me give you My higher perspective.

17

So, rest in Me, dear Sara. I love you. I do reign above it all. Above everything. Wayman's passing. His death from this physical life to eternal life. It is not darkness, but My love and mercy and compassion reign. I know what I am doing. I only know LOVE. MERCY. COMPASSION. I know you miss your Man so much. I am the great I AM. So, you are not alone. I am the I AM. I am IMMANUEL. I am with you. Be strong as I am with you. In you. For you. I am opening doors. Trust Me. I know you have surrendered to Me. My ways are higher than yours. I have your Man. I am sending angels to encamp around you. Take My word for this plan. I am helping you. Can you see Me? Can you feel Me? I am with you. Ask Me and I will tell you more.

Love, Jesus.

> Take it one day at a time.

Journal Prompt

What do you imagine God is thinking about your loss? About His timing? Tell Him your heart. He loves hearing your story. He is catching your tears.

Day 16, February 3, 2020

Good morning, Jesus. You tell me that You will give me REST. When I am weary, You will give me rest. You said, "Sara, here is a place of rest. Let the weary rest here. This is a place of quiet rest." Lord, give me Your rest. Where You are. Where You comfort me.

Isaiah 28:12 NLT

"God has told his people, 'Here is a place of rest; let the weary rest here. This is a place of quiet rest.' But they would not listen."

Jesus Stream

I am your comfort. Trust Me. Dear One. I hold it all. I AM holding you right in the middle. I am Your comfort. No one else. I am the great I AM. So go exercise and let me comfort you. You are My precious daughter. You are not alone. I am your REST. Come to Me. Keep writing. Keep processing. You are My love. Oceans of Grief. The waves crash down. Waters cover you.

Day 17, February 4, 2020, Selah, quiet interlude

Day 18, February 5, 2020, Selah, quiet interlude

Dear Jesus — fill me with hope.

Colleen sent me this scripture today.

Romans 15:13 NIV

"May the God of all hope fill you with all joy and peace as you trust in Him so that you may overflow with hope by the power of the Holy Spirit."

So, today, help me overflow with hope. I desire hope and joy and peace. Because of You, Jesus. So today, I have hope.

Journal Prompt

Do you need a hope infusion? God is ready to fill you with His joy and peace. What do you need to let go of to be filled with hope? Hope and despair cannot live side by side. Ask God to help you release despair and depression. Let His hope pour into the crevices of your soul.

> *You have permission to grieve in your own way.*

Day 19, February 6, 2020, Selah, quiet interlude

Day 20, February 7, 2020, Selah, quiet interlude

Day 21, February 8, 2020, Selah, quiet interlude

My pain was real. I was a wound of sadness. I was unable to write.

I was beginning to be able to leave my house and own space for short jaunts. I was searching for a new purpose to keep going. The reality of the new routine was overwhelming. Everything was different every single day and night. My predominant feeling was loneliness and sadness as the reality of my loss was sinking in.

Loneliness overwhelmed my heart. I was numb when among large groups of people. Life was difficult to navigate, and I realized it.

Journal Prompt

What are you realizing at this point in your grieving? Are you able to get out at all? If so, where are you going and how do you feel when there? What is your predominant feeling at this time? Is grief being replaced by numbness? If yes, how does it feel? If not, what, if anything, is replacing your grief at this moment?

> *Tomorrow is another day.*

Day 22, February 9, 2020

Yesterday I went to minister on the streets of South Congress. We did it. I passed out Your love. The strength of My Man carries me still. Michelle N. sees Wayman in charge of the vineyards. In charge of the New Wine. Pouring it out on us here on earth. I praise You, Jesus. Breakthrough is Your name. Jesus. You are coming back. It is just You, Jesus. You are ALL that matters. Lord, thank You for being my Jesus. My God. My King. New wine skin. New thinking. Let me see You in my vision. Fresh perspective. An upgrade. Lord, thank You for New Wine. New upgrades for Your plans. For me. Sara Lee Coston Thurman. For my loneliness without My Man — Wayman Lee Thurman. Lord, fill me up. You are my answer. Lord, I pick up my mat. All for you Jesus. Places and spaces You are setting up. Open the doors, Lord, for me. Favor of the Lord is mine. Peace. Power. Purity… So, Lord, use me. Teach me. Show me. Transform me. I am Yours.

Romans 8:38 NLT

"And I am convinced that nothing can ever separate us from God's love. Neither death nor life, neither angels nor demons, neither our fears for today nor our worries about tomorrow — not even the powers of hell can separate us from God's love."

Thanks, Jesus, for this promise. I am thankful.

Journal Prompt

Can you believe Romans 8:38 right now in your life circumstances? Write how it feels death is a separation of love. It is a process of believing this truth in God's Word. I pray a special prayer for you, as you have made it this far. God wants to touch your bleeding heart right now. He invites you to tell Him your pain.

Day 23, February 10, 2020

Jesus, You are with me in the middle.

ISAIAH 1:19 TPT

"If you have a willing heart to let me help you and if you will obey me, you will feast on the blessings of an abundant harvest."

So, Lord, I want to be obedient to You. To every word to Your voice of love. I respond with all of me —Your feast of abundant harvest is awaiting me. Lord, pour Your strength into me. Thank You, Jesus.

Prayer

Lord, make our hearts willing to receive Your help. Open our eyes and ears to receive the help You are sending our way. It may not be in the manner we thought it would come, but You are God. And this is Your promise. Help us to obey You and live to feast on the blessings of an abundant harvest.

Psalm 65:11 NLT

"You crown the year with a bountiful harvest; even the hard pathways overflow with abundance."

Journal Prompt

Do you need help? Can you tell God what you think you need?

> *Feel all the feels. It is your pathway to healing.*

Day 24, February 11, 2020

Dear Jesus, I made it through yesterday. You brought me comfort. You brought me clarity that I miss My Man. My companion. My helper. My confidant. My problem solver. So today I will paint. I will prepare for the future.

Psalm 69:3 NLT

*"My eyes are swollen with weeping,
waiting for my God to help me."*

Psalm 69:29 NLT

*"I am suffering and in pain. Rescue me,
O God, by your saving power."*

> *Breathe in Jesus. Breathe out praise.*

Psalm 69:32 NLT

*"The humble will see their God at work and be glad.
Let all who seek God's help be encouraged."*

II Samuel 22:33 NIV

*"It is God who arms me with strength and
keeps my ways secure."*

Jesus Stream

Yes, Sara, my beautiful one, you are having to trust Me in new ways. Knowing I have gone before you in new ways. I can see it all. I hold it all together. You are not alone. I have it all worked out. Trust Me. Trust Me. Watch Me. I am your Friend! Your beautiful Friend! So today, trust Me. Watch Me. Yes. Paint. Write. I bless you, Sara Lee Coston Thurman.

Journal Prompt

How are you doing today? Can you allow any thoughts of the future? Are you able to activate some creativity in your life? Even an adult coloring book and new markers can be a place of comfort.

Day 25, February 12, 2020

Dear Jesus — Oh how my broken heart breaks even more. It bleeds. It is raw and open and painful with weeping. A broken heart with My Man gone. Lord, You let me realize the depth of his passing little by little. Not too much, but You are guiding me in the process. Thank You Lord for Your kindness. The first — turning off Wayman's phone yesterday. Oh, my that was hard. Just day by day. Step by step. Lord, I trust You today. I must trust You. You are with me. Lord, my heart is raw. These scriptures are my anchors today.

Psalm 9:10 NLT

"Those who know Your name trust in You, for You, O Lord, do not abandon those who search for You."

Isaiah 41:10 NLT

"Don't be afraid for I am with you. Don't be discouraged for I am your God. I will strengthen you and help you. I will hold you with My victorious right hand."

Jesus Stream

Oh, My dearest Sara, My beautiful one. I hold you. I am your defender. I am your high tower. Your Savior. Your hope. And love. And joy. And peace. I am your purpose. I am the I AM. I am Immanuel. I AM with you. Oh, My dearest Sara. So, let's do this. We are one. You are not alone. Not abandoned. Not alone. But at one with Me. I know Wayman Lee is not answering his phone anymore. But I Am. I hear your cries. I hear your needs. I am your provider. I will not abandon you. So come to Me, dear daughter. I am your Helper. Your Light. Your Love. I will slowly heal your broken heart. Let Me pour My salve on it. I am with you. Listen to Me. I am your strength. Your heartbeat. I am showing you more of Me than you have ever seen. Yes — it is Me. So, dance with Me. Rest in My arms. Let Me embrace You. I love you. I love you very much. So, let's dance. Watch Me. I am the lead. Together we will bring hope and love and joy. See you tell My story through yours. I love you, Sara Lee Coston Thurman, so very much. Love, Jesus.

Journal Prompt

Do you feel alone and abandoned? Tell God. Let Him embrace you. Are you beginning to feel an inkling of your new purpose in the midst of grief?

> *Deep grief is a result of deep love.*

The Most Beautiful Walk

By Sara Thurman

It was our favorite path. It was well worn. Daily, in the late afternoon, hand in hand. Out the driveway and turn left. Every time.

It was just our norm. Every day we took a walk. Very very few exceptions. Time to take a "W-A-L-K." We spelled it because the dogs drove us crazy if they had to wait even ten minutes. Communication with each other. Checking in. Was this a good time for you?

Our talk and walk could be serious. Or not. Our talk and walk could be full of dreams. Or not. Our talk and walk could be reflective. Or not. Or our walk could just be. Normal. Silent. Hand in hand. Down the path. Each with a dog. Wayman with Chico, the chihuahua. Me with Coda, the yellow lab.

This path is where our son told us about the girl he wanted to date. And now they are married. This path is where we took our last family picture together, with the phone on the cedar tree limb, a year before you left this earth.

This path is where we talked about hard things. About fun things. Happy things. We talked. We walked. We held hands. We listened. We told each other our secrets.

I miss your hand in my hand. Both dogs are gone now, too. It is not the same. Ever. But still, I take a walk. Every day. Few exceptions. Usually a different route. Because the memories are so very fresh. Still.

This path of trust. This path of love. I am forever grateful for the most beautiful walk.

February 18, 2021

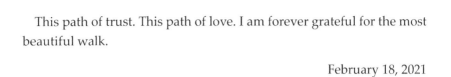

Tell the truth about your grief. It will help you heal.

Overview of Days 26 through 50

Feelings: Deep sadness settled in as my main emotion. And closely following is intense loneliness as my reality. Crashing emotions, changing frequently within every part of every day.

What I needed most:

- Continued witnessing of my grief by others around me.

- I needed others to continue to ask me how I was doing at that moment and then to take the time to listen to me.

- I was so lost in not knowing what to do every day. It was helpful for people to give me suggestions. For example, a friend came to help me write my condolence thank you notes. I needed this help as it was so very painful.

- I needed to be around people every day. I continued with my personal training at my local gym. I added a third day each week as having this routine was essential to my mental health.

- A friend to call me every evening about 9 p.m., as this was one of my loneliest times of day. No husband. Just loneliness and emptiness.

- I continued to cry many, many times each day. I needed to let the tears continue to flow.

- I needed others to call me to check in and to invite me to do things.

What I did not need:

- Anyone to tell me the first year is the worst.

- Someone to ask me how I was doing and not take the time to listen to my answer.

- Isolation or to be alone.

- Others thought I was not grieving correctly. It was new territory for me, and there is no right or wrong way to grieve. I needed to do it my way, not the way someone else did it or thought I should do it.

Transitions I was aware of during this time:

- Hope was beginning to rise over despair in parts of some days.

- I was searching for new purposes in life and was struggling to find them.

- I needed to have new ways of coping with change and stress since Wayman was not available as my anchor.

> Tears are your best friend. God made you to cry, so cry.

Day 26, February 13, 2020

Dear Jesus, Thank You for this gorgeous day. Grounded in truth. Taking inventory. Who are You, God? Are You trustworthy?

Trust Him. Pour through me. God is going to bless them. Realness that is OK! Find your people. Worship — call out to God — praising Him. Speak the lyrics out.

I Peter 5:7 TPT

"For He always tenderly cares for you."

Psalm 27:14 TPT

"...be brave and courageous, and never lose hope."

James 5:16 NLT

"Confess your sins to each other and pray for each other so that you may be healed."

Journal Prompt

Do you feel scattered? Not able to think through a decision or thought? Just breathe in today. Be ok. Let out your real and random thoughts, prayers, and praises.

Day 27, February 14, 2020, Selah, quiet interlude

Day 28, February 15, 2020

Oh Lord Jesus — I love You. Today, I will go eat lunch with friends. I sit with You. I washed the dishes. I straightened up. Later today I will finish my thank you notes. For people who have given with grace and generosity, I am so blessed. Yesterday was Valentine's Day — My Man was celebrated at graveside. I miss you so much, Wayman, but I know I have an everlasting love. That will never ever end. My heart is blessed, Jesus.

Jeremiah 31:3 NLT

"I have loved you, my people, with an everlasting love. With unfailing love, I have drawn you to Myself."

So, Lord, I know this kind of love. It will never end with You. It will only keep going — so thanks, God, for the revelation of this kind of love. I want to receive it from You. Only You. Lord. My Lover. My Provider. My Protector. My God. My Friend. So now I listen.

Jesus Stream

Oh, My dearest Sara, you are doing well. So, well. One day at a time. One step. One minute. But your eyes are fixed on Me. I love you so much. I gave you the best husband. I gave you Wayman Lee Thurman. What a journey you have had. It was beautiful and holy and precious. I am so blessed by your obedience. Your love. Your strength. Your bravery. Your love for Me. So, my beautiful one, My daughter. Each step is beautiful. Keep taking the steps. I am the I AM — I am with you. I know you. I hold you dear. I love you. I am your Provider. Keep being obedient. Soaking into Me. Leaning on Me. Where you are weak, and I am strong. Oh, my beautiful Sara. Stay strong. By leaning on Me. I catch your tears. I love you so much. This day is glorious. I am with you.

> Tears release toxins and bring peace to your soul. So, cry.

Journal Prompt

What are some characteristics of your loved one that you miss the most? It has been four weeks since your loved one has transitioned from your earthly reality. What does everlasting love look like to you?

Day 29, February 16, 2020

Oh, Jesus —Thank You for helping me write over fifty thank you notes. Today, over forty personal notes of Your Kingdom coming to earth in the form of love and thanksgiving. Thank You for many who have prayed and are STILL praying for me. Thank You for the saints. Wayman, talk to me. Angels be messengers to me from My Man. I miss him. I can't think about it too much. As I can't breathe. I can't talk. Oh, Jesus, this loss is great. I am overwhelmed. It is more than I can take. Until I stop. And say, Jesus. Your name. You say You are with me when I walk through the darkest valley. You are with me.

"Even when your path takes me through the valley of deepest darkness, fear will never conquer me, for You already have! Your authority is my strength and my peace. The comfort of Your love takes away my fear. I'll never be lonely, for you are near."

Psalm 91:1 TPT

"You are hidden in the strength of the God Most High."

Psalm 91:10 TPT

"...our secret hiding place, we will always be shielded from harm."

Do I believe that? Oh, God. Comfort me. Shield me.

Psalm 23:4 TPT

"Even when Your path takes me through the valley of deepest darkness, fear will never conquer me..."

You remain close to me and lead me all the way through it.

Jesus Stream

Do you really believe Me, Sara? I am with you. I have everything planned out. If you don't make it to these certain criteria, it is ok. I can see it ALL. I hold it ALL together. You are a world changer. I am in charge of your release, not man. So, wait on Me. Wait.

Psalm 46:10 NLT

"Be still, and know I am God!"

I know what to open and what to close. Trust Me, dear one. You are in the river of life.

Ezekiel 47:9 NLT

"...life will flourish wherever this river flows."

Release control to Me. It is ALL mine. My glory will be known. Eyes fixed on Me. What you see and believe. What you hear and believe. I will give you a message. I will tell you. Faith in Me, dear one. It will be from Me. Not from you. So just listen. Wait. Be still. I will come. It is Psalm 23. Just wait. The taxes. I will help you. The writing. I will help you. The painting. I will help you. I am your strength. I am holding your hand. So just be with Me. I love you. Go water your garden. Then paint. Then walk. Then write. Just enjoy Me today. I love you, Sara.

Love, Jesus

Journal Prompt

Are you overwhelmed in your grief? Tell Jesus. Ask Him to give you one step to do. For me, as noted in my journal entry, it was to release His name out loud. Over and over, just say, "Jesus. Jesus. Jesus."

Can you find a few scriptures that minister to your heart and give you hope? Write them down. Read them out loud. Maybe color them. Make a piece of art out of them with colored pencils or markers.

Is God telling you to wait on something? There is so, so much to do. Ask God to help you with the next step on the next thing. He will.

Day 30, February 17, 2020, Selah, quiet interlude

Day 31, February 18, 2020, Selah, quiet interlude

Oh, the walk is harder than I knew. Harder ground than I knew was possible. But You, God, are with me. Thanks for sending help. Thanks for Justin's phone calls. Thanks for Jordan checking on me. Thanks to Ann for reaching out. Thanks for it all. Thanks for Judy's lunch and Ann's late-night talks and visits. For Kim's scripture emails. Thanks, God. Thanks so much for being You. Being God. A God I trust. A God I know. A God I can count on. A God fighting my battles. A God on my side. A God giving me strength. A God walking by my side, holding my hand in the valley of the shadow of death.

Oh, God — You are my Friend. My true Friend. My Confidant. My Joy. My Peace. My God. Day 31. Oh God — how much longer will my broken heart bleed? How much longer will I feel like I can't breathe? I have huge waves of pain crashing on me with such force and strength; they take my breath away. I don't know which side is up. Then I feel Your Presence. You just sit with me. You wait for me. You just love me. You don't try to fix it. You just are. With. Me. Forever. I can feel Your love. Your message of hope. Your thankfulness for My Man. For his life of service. Lived with honor, gentleness, kindness, joy, and strength.

Jesus Stream

Job well done, My son. You ran the race. You won. You are home. You have received your prize. Eternal life. FOREVER. With. Me. The I AM.

So, we wait for the day of Awakening. The day in history when Heaven meets earth. The day when tears are washed away. When tears are no more. Yes, that day of re — unity. Re — union. When all pain is gone. Communion. So, today, I give you strength. Joy. Peace. Hope. And ALL of My LOVE.

Journal Prompt

What is the hardest part of Day 31 that you are now walking through? Tell God what hurts the most and what the hardest thing is today. Is it the seen or unseen rocks that seem most treacherous? Expect the most difficult things to change from day to day. It is similar to hurricane strength waves crashing on what was just hours before a calm and serene beach. Can you relate to the crashing waves?

Can you find one verse or one thought to hold onto that brings you comfort or hope in this season of deep grief? Ask God to whisper His love song over you in your brokenness.

Day 32, February 19, 2020, Selah, quiet interlude

Day 33, February 20,2020

Oh, Jesus, You know the tears I've already shed. Through the night. My Man. My Wayman would have celebrated eighty-two years old today. My heart is thankful. So thankful for this man You created. The world is changing because of him. More love. More service. My thankfulness. I am so thankful for this man. My husband. The father of our sons, a friend to many. Enjoying the simple life. Joy. Peace. Gentleness. Kindness. So thankful for who Wayman was. Husband of my dreams. He was so amazing. Thank You, Lord, for our life together. The rotten apples. And the good spots. The good times. The beautiful life. Oh, how I miss him. Lord, help me grasp more of heaven. More of You in these days. In this time. Sometimes, Wayman would say, "Just live with it." So, no fretting. Just loving others. Peaceful and solid and steady. My Facebook post at 2 a.m. tells it best, "Oh Jesus, comfort my heart today. Hide me in the folds of Your robe. I am so blessed. You are my Defender. I know that in new ways. You have my back. You are making the way. Lord, I love You. Papa God, thank You for loving me so well. For literally surrounding me. So, thanks for this man. My Man. Oh, I miss him. Two things I know and believe:

1. Your beautiful mercy took Wayman home into fullness of health.

2. Wayman's days and purposes on earth were fulfilled. He ran his race and finished so well.

Thank You. Thank You. Thank You for creating him. Wayman Lee Thurman. For planning who he was. To love You and to love others so well.

> *I need to feel the pain to get through the pain.*

The Rotten Apple Story, Circa 2000

I was a very busy working mom with two sons, Jordan and Justin, in elementary school. Actually, I was the Assistant Principal of their school and also in graduate school, working on my doctorate degree at the University of Houston. Wayman was working in software sales at this time which required a lot of traveling. My schedule was such that I did not buy the groceries regularly for our family. Or if I did, it was a rare occurrence. My Man was the grocery shopper for our family. He would find the time in his week to go buy food for us to eat and to serve us.

The fruit we regularly ate in our home was apples and bananas. On more than one occasion, I complained to Wayman about the brown soft spots on the apples. On the rare occasions I went to the store, I would carefully look over each piece of fruit. When Wayman bought fruit, he would just put them in the bag without inspection and move on to the next item on his list.

I regularly complained and pointed out the rotting spots on the apples and asked Wayman why he would buy rotten apples. He grew tired of my negative talk and at some point, asked me if I wanted to start buying groceries every week. It was a big wake-up call for me.

I realized I was concentrating on the rotten spots instead of cutting off those spots and enjoying the rest of the healthy apple. I learned a big lesson in these acts of service for our family from My Man. We had apples to eat. We can look at the negative or we can look at the good. My Man taught me so much by his example of service to our family. We had apples to eat. Just get the knife and cut off the rotten spots and throw them in the trash. And enjoy the remaining delicious fruit with happiness and gratitude. This metaphor for life is a beautiful example of where my heart needs to be focused. My Man taught me so much over thirty-four years. I am so grateful.

Jesus Stream

The new heaven and the new earth.

Isaiah 66:18 TPT

"They will come and gaze upon my radiance."

Oh, My dear Sara. My beautiful one. You are loved. You are planned. I am holding you dear one. I am your strength. Your joy. Your peace. Let me breathe on you. I love you with an everlasting love, like I love Wayman. He is with Me. In fullness of health. Planning and helping Me. Create new. Yes, you are loving him well. His memory. His family. His ways. I created him to create. And that he did. Oh, what joy you and your Man had. My joy awaits those who keep their eyes on me.

Hebrews 12:2 NLT

"Keeping our eyes on Jesus, the pioneer and perfecter of our faith. For the joy that lay before Him, He endured the cross, despising the shame."

Nehemiah 8:10 NLT

"...the joy of the Lord is your strength."

Such purposes remain in your life to share and love and release My goodness. I love you, dear one. You are My precious one. I am helping you. Read about the talents. I have this message for the ladies. Get those note cards done. I have the words. I love you. I love you. I love you. I am your strength. High tower. Rock. Joy. Peace. Provider. I love you. You are not alone. I am holding it all together. I am that I am. I love you, My darling. Oh, so much.

Love, Jesus

Journal Prompt

What is your cry in the middle of the night? What is your greatest need at this hour? On this day? Tell God. And tell someone else who can help you during this most intense time of loss as reality settles into loneliness.

Day 34, February 21, 2020, Selah, quiet interlude

Day 35, February 22, 2020

Dear Jesus — How beautiful You are. Lord, I give up control to You. Lord, come to me. Let me release to You, my control. Jesus. I am weak. You are strong. You are my King. My God. My One and Only, Lord. Let it be. Let me relax into Your arms. All that I love is Yours, Lord God. And all You have is mine. I am Your daughter. So, there is plenty. Abundance. Oh, Jesus. Only You. Help me. Oh, when I get stressed, how I want My Man. I miss Wayman so much. Oh Lord, Jesus I miss Wayman Lee Thurman. Will You come to me? Will You come to comfort my heart?

Lord, help me to find Your smooth places. No rough potholes.

Jeremiah 31:13 NLT

"I will turn their mourning into joy. I will comfort them and exchange their sorrow for rejoicing."

Oh, Lord, I wait for this day.

Jesus Stream

My dearest daughter, I breathe peace on you. Breath Me in. I am your stream of living waters. Give me control of your mind. I am yours. You are Mine. We are one. You can trust Me. I am the Great I Am.

Jeremiah 31:3 NLT

"I have loved you with an everlasting love. I have loved you with unfailing love. I have drawn you to Myself."

Journal Prompt

Ask God for a verse or passage that brings truth right to your heart, mind, and soul like Jeremiah 31:9 did for me. Write and pray this scripture as truth for your soul.

Day 36, February 23, 2020, Selah, quiet interlude

Day 37, February 24, 2020, Selah, quiet interlude

Day 38, February 25, 2020, Selah, quiet interlude

Day 39, February 26, 2020, Selah, quiet interlude

Day 40, February 27, 2020, Selah, quiet interlude

Day 41, February 28, 2020

Oh, Jesus, how You love me. Your eyes are on me. You have sent Helpers this week. Gifts of love. Mary Lou visiting me! Wow! Thanks, God. Then I went to Trader Joe's on Tuesday because I heard You tell me to go. I received love there. Hugs and ten additional sunflowers.

Sunflowers at Trader Joe's

I dropped off my friend, Mary Lou, at the Austin airport and then felt an urgency to go to Trader Joe's to shop for a few groceries. Trader Joe's is not a place Wayman and I shopped regularly, and, in fact, I had never been to this exact store before. It was a stressful parking situation with very tight parking spots in a covered garage with little signage on how to navigate the ordeal. I was in tears by the time I parked and even considered going home without the items I needed. My drive home is about an hour from Trader Joe's.

I spent more than an hour walking up and down the aisles checking out all the different foods. It felt like I was in a state of numbness, and I actually lost track of time. I saw the flowers and knew I needed to purchase sunflowers because they stay fresh for a while and were symbolic of hope in the midst of my grief.

When it came time to check out, I chose a line with a male checker. He was very cheery and asked how I was doing. Waves of intense sadness rolled over me. I broke down crying and explained my husband had passed away in January. He was extremely kind and gracious. I then made my way out of the store and realized I needed to get my parking ticket validated. Just then, as I was standing near the machine, the cashier came running out of the store with a large bunch of fresh sunflowers and handed them to me as a gift. I immediately felt the love of God by this gesture. I felt seen and loved. And boy, did I have fun when I arrived home, finding places for all twenty of my fresh giant sunflowers. This simple gesture of kindness helped me to not feel so alone in my grief on this particular day.

Journal Prompt

Who has God sent you in the way of Helpers so far? Know that more are coming! God can see your needs before you ask Him. Ask Him for more Helpers in your time of needs

Day 42, February 29, 2020

Then…New Day, Bonus Day. Extra day in February.

Thank You, Jesus. You are with me. I know it.

Jude 1-2 NLT

I am writing to all who have been called by God the Father, who loves you and keeps you safe in the care of Jesus Christ! May God give you more and more mercy, peace and love."

Journal Prompt

Can you say, "Thank You, Jesus!" today? Ask God for more and more mercy, peace, and love today. Write a prayer.

Day 43, March 1, 2020

Lord Jesus, I don't seem to get very far when it comes to being focused and on task. To journal. Lord, I am broken hearted. Lonely. Oh, how I miss My Man. My anchor. My heart. My love. My Man. How can I go on? It seems like I can't keep going forward at times. But I know Your promises of comfort even in my deep grief. My grief is so painful. I can feel my bones and my heart are bleeding because My Man left earth to go home to You.

I am thankful he is Home. He is whole. He is healed. He is with You. Totally and fully. He gave me so much, Jesus. Help me to multiply what You have given me. I am honored to be Wayman's wife. Lord, what a lonely road after being one with him. So alone. So, come, great I Am.

Help me bring glory to You. All eyes to You, King Jesus. Not to me, but to You as my Helper and King. My Comfort. My Purpose. My Grace. My Love. My Life. My Art. My Writing. My Blogs. My Video on IGTV. Lord, this is You. Oh, my dear Jesus. You are helping me. You have my tears in the bottle. The tears I have shed You have bottled.

Psalm 56:8 NLT

"You keep track of all of my sorrows. You have collected all my tears in Your bottle. You have recorded each one in Your book."

Lord, I want to ponder all Your deeds in the midst of my grief.

Psalm 111:2 NLT

"How amazing are the deeds of the Lord! All who delight in Him should ponder them."

Help me to praise You always. Even more, since Wayman's race is WON. Help me to praise You, O Jesus. Holy Spirit come and comfort my grief. Father, God, help me to trust You.

Jesus Stream

Oh, My daughter, you are so loved. You are doing well. You are riding the waves of loss. You loved your man so well. I am so proud of you, dear beautiful one. My darling Sara — keep on taking the next steps. It may feel like you are not moving forward, but you are.

I am working behind the scenes. I know you know that. Just wait. Just rest in Me. Just snuggle into My arms. I am holding you. I am using you for My glory. I know you are doing hard things. You are pressing into the hard. Into the pain. Not skirting around it. But plowing right through the pain. I am so proud of you. I am your Defender. Your Helper. Your Comfort. Your Purpose. Your Provider. Don't you see how I helped you with taxes. I am expanding your money. I have you. Keep moving forward. Keep on keeping on. I see you. I am working all things out.

43

Ponder My deeds. Psalm 111:2. Last week I sent you ten extra sunflowers. I sent you $500 in an anonymous money order. I took care of your Long-Term Care for the remainder of your life. I helped you sell over $1,000 of art. I helped you get a connection to a non-profit for you to donate your art. I set up an opportunity for you to teach at a retreat out of state. Yes, daughter, I have you. I am watching over you. I am so proud of your choices. Of your love for Me. Of your love for your family. Your kids. Your grandchildren. For your friends. Yes, dear one, I am with you. Every detail is Mine. I have gone before you. Watch Me. In wonder and awe. You believe. You keep the Faith. The Joy. I am using you to the ends of the earth. Let's get this worked out. I am Your Helper. You are not done. Let's do this sweet and beautiful daughter. Together, we can bring light into darkness. Much, much love. You are My shining light. My delight. My voice of authenticity. Don't let jealousy or comparison creep in. Each person is unique. Stay in your lane. I love you. I love you. I protect you. Keep on loving Me and loving others. I love you so much. You are doing so well... My brave and fierce warrior princess.

Love always, Jesus

P.S. You know I have sent an array of angels to be around you. You are surrounded. But don't speed, dear one. I am protecting you. Follow My guidance. Trust Me in new ways.

Journal Prompt

Lord, here are some ways I need to be focused. My mind is all over the place. Will You give me Your "to do" list? I feel so scattered. That is my reality. Help me focus on what I have to do and release what I do not have to do today.

What do *you* need to focus on now? What things have you let slide due to your grief? Can you pick those things up now? If not, what can you do today to help you move toward picking those things up in the future?

Write a prayer to God about His perspective of your loved one's passing. Ask Him for His perspective. My own perspective is so very sad and like a cut off limb. I need You, God!

This is my prayer to you, God.

Help me to praise You always. Even more, for Wayman's race is WON. Help me to praise You, O Jesus. Holy Spirit come and comfort my grief. Father, God, help me to trust You.

Can you write a prayer, or use mine, filling in your loved one's name? If so, what would you write? Share it with God. Share it with a loved one and ask them to pray it with you.

Day 44, March 2, 2020, Selah, quiet interlude

Day 45, March 3, 2020, Selah, quiet interlude

Day 46, March 4, 2020, Selah, quiet interlude

Day 47, March 5, 2020

Dear Jesus, I want to live for You. To lock arms with You.

I Timothy 1:5 NLT

"The purpose of my instruction is that all believers would be filled with love that comes from a pure heart, a clear conscience, and genuine faith."

All believers would:

1. Be filled with love that comes from a pure heart

2. Have a clear conscience

3. Have genuine faith.

Oh, Lord, it feels like I need more than You. I miss My Man so much. I will sing and praise You, My Lord & God. The beauty of Holiness. Praise the Lord, for His mercy endures forever.

II Chronicles 20:21-22 NLT

"After consulting the people, the king appointed singers to walk ahead of the army, singing to the LORD and praising him for his holy splendor. This is what they sang:

'Give thanks to the LORD; His faithful love endures forever!'

At the very moment they began to sing and give praise, the Lord caused the armies of Ammon, Moab, and Mount Seir to start fighting among themselves."

Lord, I will praise You today. Surprise me today. Lord, I love You. I praise Your holiness. You are enough for me. God Almighty. I am blessed to know You. You are beautiful. Today, take my mind and bless me. Take my time. My place. My space. Oh, Jesus. I love You, Jesus. Help me to praise You. To love You with a pure heart. Nothing for me. Only You, Sweet God. I love You. I sing praises to You. My eyes are fixed on You. Not on me. I receive from You, O, Lord.

> *There is not a wrong way to grieve.*

Jesus Stream

Yes, daughter. Keep your eyes on Me. One look. Keep looking up. Fix your eyes. I am holding you, dear one. I am surrounding you. I am proud of you. You are helping others. It is about Me. My love. My peace. My joy. My faith. You can grab it. How I love you and yes — I want you to grasp the spiritual sense of each (emotion) to be completed in Me in new ways. The five senses: eyes to see, ears to hear, nose to smell, tongue to taste, skin to touch. I will release more to you. Be strong in Me. I love you!

Jesus

Journal Prompt

Do you realize the depth of what praise does for us on the battlefield? Can you praise God in new ways today? Do you have a favorite play list or worship song? Can you sing out loud? Something happens in the atmosphere when we praise God in song.

Write about a surprise you would love from God today. Can you give God your mind today?

Day 48, March 6, 2020, Selah, quiet interlude

Day 49, March 7, 2020, Selah, quiet interlude

Day 50, March 8, 2020, Selah, quiet interlude

Overview of Days 51 through 75

Feelings: Increased peace and acceptance of Wayman's passing. Sadness is still a dominant feeling. Less numbness and increased knowledge of my new purpose in this new season.

What I needed most:

- To realize I could make it, one day at a time. If I stayed in the present hour, I would be ok. If I thought too much about the future, I did not function in peace.

- To praise God by writing, creating, singing, and declaring His goodness. I knew when I praised God with song or words, my heart felt more peaceful.

- To be able to cry, every day. This was my new normal of being a grieving widow.

What I did not need:

- To be told that next year would still be horrible.

- Being asked how I was doing and then not taking the time to listen to my answer.

- For friends and loved ones to stop calling and checking on me or inviting me to an outing. I need this now more than ever.

- To think or be told I was not grieving correctly.

Transitions I noticed during this time:

- I continued to have days where I couldn't think but I could feel more purpose emerging in my soul.

- I continued to search for new purposes in life and was feeling more peaceful about God's provision.

- I began to understand the plans of God for Wayman in a greater way. I continued to learn to release Wayman into God's arms in new ways of acceptance.

Day 51, March 9, 2020, Selah, quiet interlude

Day 52, March 10, 2020, Selah, quiet interlude

Day 53, March 11, 2020

So much. So much. So many tears. My heart is broken. Oh, how I miss My Man. Lord, You know. But You. But You. My Lord. My God. My Shelter. My Provider. My King. My Savior. My Purpose. Thanks. Help me to help others. Lord, I am there in the middle of this grief. Or only at the beginning? But You, God. Help me. You are sending others to help me. Thanks.

Psalms 139:4-5 NLT

"You know what I am going to say even before I say it, Lord. You go before me and follow me. You place Your hand of blessing on my head."

Jesus Stream

Yes, My dear one, Sara Lee Coston Thurman. I am with you, dear one. My darling. My beautiful one. I am with you. I am holding you tightly. I know you are in pain. Deep grief.

Journal Prompt

Can you believe even a tiny part of this promise that God has gone before you? Can you receive a blessing today from God? God already knows your thoughts of despair and grief today. Can you tell Him anyway? God is going before you, minute by minute, hour by hour, and day by day. Take a deep breath and say, " I can make it for the next minute. I can make it for the next hour. I can make it for today."

Day 54, March 12, 2020, Selah, quiet interlude

Day 55, March 13, 2020, Selah, quiet interlude

Day 56, March 14, 2020

Oh Lord Jesus - You are my strength. My Help. My Anchor. Thanks so much dear one. Today I woke up. My tears have not yet come like rivers. Last night I cried and groaned and burst my heart open to You. I miss My Man so much. I can't breathe at times. Oh, I miss him. My Wayman Lee Thurman. I miss you. I made it through the week. I miss you. I miss you. My heart aches because you are not here. I miss you.

So, I thank You, dear Jesus, for this place. My home. It is peaceful. It is safe. It is from You. I am so thankful. I bring my heart to You, O Lord. I am not alone. You are with me, O Jesus. You are my safe place. Oh, Lord - You are with me. I am so blessed. Safe. Warm. Perfect home. Everything I need, plus more. O Jesus. Thank You.

Jesus Stream

Isaiah 55:11-13 NLT

"It is the same with My Word. I send it out and it always produces fruit. It will accomplish all I want it to, and it will prosper everywhere I send it. You will live in joy and peace... These events will bring great honor to the Lord's name; they will be an everlasting sign of His power and love."

Yes, My dearest Sara Lee Coston Thurman. I am weaving your story. It is beautiful. It is good. I Am the I Am. Hummingbirds are here. I sent my birds to encourage you. To bless you. I am using you to plant seeds. More than you can see. I am holding you. Yes. I am your anchor. Rest, and watch Me work in your life. I will produce fruit. It is all eyes on Me. You are my beautiful willing servant. I am the source. The plans are Mine. I will accomplish more. I will prosper you everywhere I send you. You will live in joy and peace.

Yes, you are ready for spring. Did you notice how I made the day of Wayman's service 68 degrees in January? I honor him. Yes, he was your anchor. But I had his days numbered. It was My mercy and love for him that I took/brought him home. My darling, Sara, you are doing well. Lean into Me. I am your Anchor. Your strength. Your peace. Your joy. I am the source of beauty and love. You have everything you need. You have Me. I know your heart aches. Broken. Bleeding. But, dear one, I am with you in new ways, I am your Defender. I release a new provision for you. Books, retreats, speaking engagements, paintings. Dear Sara, I have it all. I will make it happen step by step. Rest in Me. Come into My arms, Trust Me. No worries. So, My darling. My Beautiful One. Watch Me. Talk to Me. Come to Me. I am your strength. Your joy. Your people. Keep breathing. Keep putting one step in front of the other.

Journal Prompt

What are you most worried about? Can you give it to Jesus? Can you lay it at His beautiful feet? Can you hear His words of encouragement? Assurance? His plan for your future? Ask God for help to not worry and for assurance that He will take care of you and your needs.

Day 57, March 15, 2020

Dear Jesus. It is hard. So hard. Oh, dear Lord, Help me. Let me hear your voice of reason and love and strength. Lord, I need You so much. I am weak. Weary. Sad. Refresh me. Oh, Lord, my heart is weary. I miss Wayman Lee Thurman so very much. I can't breathe. I can't stand the pain. Such a deep grief to my heart. Lord, help me cope. Help me grieve. Well. Whatever that means. I really don't know. Minute by minute. Hour by hour. Day by day.

Yesterday, the hummingbirds came. The precious little tuxedo male. So quick. So precious.

(At this time God began showing me new purposes for my life, such as starting a podcast and showing me what I was to include in the podcast. I am sharing my story about taking the next steps in whatever that may be — a business, creativity, family. You will find your story inside of mine. You were created to create, and you must take the next step, too.)

So, Lord, help me with the next steps for my podcast ideas. You just gave me the assignment of starting a podcast less than two weeks ago. "Small Beginnings with Sara." I know I want to talk about grief. My tears and the different kinds of tears You created our body with the difference between tears of grief and joy and even onion tears. I want to share some daily helpful tidbits You have given me to cope with losing Wayman.

Psalms 89:15, 17 NLT

"Happy are those who hear the joyful call to worship, for they will walk in the light of your presence, Lord. You are their glorious strength. It pleases you to make us strong."

My response to this scripture was: So, Lord, I worship You. I praise you. You are my strength. I come into Your presence. And I sing and dance. I praise You, O Lord. Fill me up.

Jesus Stream

Sara, My darling. Yes, praise Me. Worship Me. Give Me thanks. I am your strength. Your purpose. Your joy. Your peace. No one can take My place. I am your anchor. Fix your eyes on Me. I am your provider. Protector. Salvation. I can do everything you need. I am never leaving you. I am your rest. Your details. Your business. Your art. So come hang with Me. You can trust Me. See, I know where Wayman is and what he is doing. He is a saint to me. I will pour my oil of gladness into your heart of mourning. Praise Me. I am NEVER leaving you. I am your strength. I love coming alive within you. I am the Great I AM. Watch Me. Learn from Me.

Journal Prompt

Do you feel any purpose for your life from God? Ask Him to give you a lifeline. Some glimmer of hope for a renewed purpose if you have not been able to see purpose in the last few months. Make a list of possible purposes for your life.

Do you feel abandoned? Can you write a prayer to Jesus telling Him that you know He will never leave you or forsake you? Stand on this promise of Jesus being your strength.

Day 58, March 16, 2020, Selah, quiet interlude

Note: I moved to Medina, Texas to be with my son, daughter-in-law, and baby granddaughter on March 16, 2020. Living alone in the midst of a pandemic was too difficult for my heart. I moved in with them not knowing for how long but knowing being at home alone during this time was not helpful or healthy.

Day 59, March 17, 2020, Selah, quiet interlude

Day 60, March 18, 2020

Dear Jesus, help me today to be full of peace and confidence in You. You are my King. My strength and peace. I need You, dear Jesus. Breathe on me. Sweet Jesus.

Habakkuk 2:4 NLT

"But the righteous will live by their faithfulness to God."

Jesus Stream

O dear one. Keep your eyes on Me. I am your strength and hope. Believe in Me. I release through you My faith and hope and love! You are My delight. I rejoice over you with singing. Love, Jesus

Journal Prompt

What do you need from Jesus today? Tell Him. He will come to your rescue. Ask Him for more faith. I bless you today on your journey.

Day 61, March 19, 2020, Selah, quiet interlude

Day 62, March 20, 2020

Dear Jesus, I hear You telling me, "Do not be afraid." You are with me. I am excited to be with You in the throne room. I trust You, Jesus. Let me hear You. I can trust You.

Jesus Stream

Welcome. Come on in. All I have is yours. Everything. Everything. No worries. I Am the I Am. The Provider. Trust Me. Jesus. Papa God. Holy Spirit.

Journal Prompt

Is there a place fear is trying to land in your heart and mind? Write about this fear and tell Jesus about it. Declare that as a son or daughter of the King of Kings, you have everything you need. Pray and talk to Jesus as if you are sitting on the couch together. He really is that close to you. You have access to Jesus twenty-four hours a day.

Day 63, March 21, 2020

Oh Jesus, how did I live without You? You are my source of joy and peace. My light. My life. Reign on earth. There are thousands and thousands of angels singing.

Revelation 5:10-11 NLT

"And you have caused them to become a Kingdom of priests for our God. And they will reign on the earth. Then I looked again,

and I heard the voices of thousands and millions of angels around the throne and of the living beings and the elders."

Jesus Stream

Yes, keep worshipping Me! Eyes on Me. Prayer and thanksgiving. Praises. Singing. Thankfulness. All help is yours from heaven. Keep creating new books and songs and art and courses. All with the purpose to draw people to Me. Yes, daughter. I celebrate with you. I Am the I Am. I am worthy of all praise. Keep on keeping on. I love you. I sing to you. Oh yes! I am Jesus. Trust Me with everything! Everything! I am your provider. I am your wisdom. Watch and wait. I am the light.

I love you, Jesus

> *You don't need fixing.*

Journal Prompt

What is Jesus telling you? Can you hear Him singing over you? What song is He singing? I pray you can experience some tangible love from Jesus, from His heart to yours. Write a prayer of thanksgiving. You have made it two months past your great loss.

Day 64, March 22, 2020

My granddaughter, Hepzibah, is one year old today. Thank You, Jesus, for this little delight. This gift of joy. Of peace. Jesus, I praise You. I worshipped music from the Upper Room today. My praise is Your praise. Lord, I thank you for all things. This time with Justin and Ana and Lillian. Thank You, Jesus. These are the days when I praise You, Jesus. Coronavirus is running around the world, infecting people. But You, O God are sovereign. You have me surrounded. I am not alone. My older son says to stay with his brother. I am safe here. I praise You, God. You are my King. I can TRUST You. I will trust You.

Your Word is to go out when You shake things. I am shaken. Wayman is not here to celebrate our beautiful granddaughter this side of heaven. I have to trust You, God.

Haggai 2:6-9, 19 NLT

"For this is what the Lord of Heaven's Armies says: In just a little while I will again shake the heavens and the earth, the oceans and the dry land. I will shake all the nations, and the treasures of all the nations will be brought to this Temple. I will fill this place with glory, says the Lord of Heaven's Armies. The silver is mine, and the gold is mine, says the Lord of Heaven's Armies. The future glory of this Temple will be greater than its past glory, says the Lord of Heaven's Armies. And in this place, I will bring peace. I, the Lord of Heaven's Armies, have spoken!"

"I am giving you a promise now while the seed is still in the barn. You have not yet harvested your grain, and your grapevines, fig trees, pomegranates, and olive trees have not yet produced their crops. But from this day onward I will bless you."

Then the promise of this from **Haggai 2:19**. Thank You, Jesus, for the steps of Your promise found in this passage of scripture.

God, this is what You have shown me, step by step, from these scriptures in **Haggai 2:4-9 NLT.**

1. *"Be strong. Be strong all you people still left on the land. Still left on earth."*

2. *"Now, get to work, for I am with you,"* says the Lord of Heaven's Armies.

3. *"My Spirit remains among you, just as I promised."*

4. *"Do not be afraid."*

5. *"I will shake the heavens, the earth, the oceans, and the dry land. I will shake all the nations."* Oh, Lord, I am shaken with Wayman gone.

6. *"I will fill this place with glory."*

7. *"The silver is mine. The gold is mine."*

8. *"The future glory will be greater than the past glory."*

9. *"And in this place, I will bring peace. I, the Lord of Heaven's Armies, have spoken."*

Lord, I receive this promise. I am giving you a promise now while the seed is still in the barn. You have not yet harvested your grain and your grapevines, fig trees, pomegranates, olive trees have not yet produced their crops. But from this day onwards I will bless you.

Jesus Stream

Oh, My daughter, you have this. I am watching over you. You are resting in Me. Do not strive. Just hang out with Me. I am holding everything together. I am your strength. You put everything as glory to Me. Now, rest from social media. Come away with Me to rest. To sing. To dance. To work out. To create. Oh, yes! I love you. You will know your next steps. You can trust Me. I am your provider.

Journal Prompt

What can you thank God for today? What is in your hand that God has given you? Praise Him. Sing a new song you have never heard before. What do you hear God singing over you? He is singing a new song of His eternal love. How can you rest in God's spirit today? How can you create rest and peace in his presence?

Day 65, March 23, 2020, Selah, quiet interlude

Day 66, March 24, 2020

You knew how hard it would be. But God, I have been back home for just one hour. It was a sweet day. But the house is empty. I know I am to be away from home again. In Medina, with my son and family for more time. Thank You, Lord. Life is so hard without Wayman. I am thankful for Justin and Ana and baby Lilian. Oh, Jesus. Thank You. You are my rock and anchor.

Psalm 23:4 NLT

"Even though I walk through the darkest valley, I will not be afraid, for You are close beside me. Your goodness and unfailing love will pursue me all the days of my life."

Jesus Stream

Really, daughter. I am going before you. Everything I have is yours. Your income taxes will be completed this week. "M" is part of My defense team. I am holding you. You are tucked into My side. You are not alone. I am breaking open new territory. I am Your Helper. I am sending you help. Yes. You are amazing. I am opening doors, new places of influence, just for you. Come on. Just rest in Me. Listen to Me. Sit with Me. We have this dear one. I am on the Throne. Oh, what a beautiful day. I am with you.

Journal Prompt

What is the hardest thing right now? Tell God what the darkest valley looks and feels like for you today. Do you need to reach out for help in a certain area? God is ready to send you help.

Day 67, March 25, 2020

Dear Jesus, You hold the whole world in Your hands. Oh, Jesus. Help me. Oh, dear Jesus. Organize my thoughts and my processes. I need clarity and focus. I love You, Lord. So be my Helper and Guide. You are the Beautiful One.

Psalm 27:14 TPT

Don't give up; don't be impatient; be entwined as one with the Lord. Be brave and courageous, and never lose hope. Yes, keep on waiting—for He will never disappoint you!"

When I am entwined around You, Jesus, I can do all things. You lead the way. So much safety with You, Jesus.

Jesus Stream

You have everything you need. I hide you in My holiness. I am snuggled into the secret place. So, Sara, stay with Me. I AM helping you every single day. Always. Day and night! So, stay with Me. I have you. So, enjoy. Be protected, dear one!

Journal Prompt

What are you most afraid of? What is hard right now? Tell Jesus. Imagine Jesus holding you so very close, entwined to Him.

Day 68, March 26, 2020

Oh, Jesus, I am so in love with You. You have me entwined with You. I am hidden in the secret place. Thank You, Lord, for today. Lord, teach me. Show me. Guide me. I am Yours. Today I am working on writing my *Small Beginnings* prayer journal and podcast information.

You have given me renewed purposes in this season, even in the midst of grieving. Only You, Lord, could do this. I am still creating with You. Today I painted an angel. So, Lord, I lay everything before You. Thanks, Jesus.

Lord, You are my leader. You are my light. My Love.

Habakkuk 2:4 NLT
"But the righteous will live by their faithfulness to God."

Lord, You are growing my faith. This scripture in Habakkuk gives me four steps to declare to You, God.

"Yet, ... I will rejoice in the Lord,
I will be joyful in the God of my salvation,
The Sovereign Lord is my strength,

He makes me as surefooted as a deer, able to tread on heights."

Ok, Jesus. I will rejoice, be joyful! I will become more surefooted and be able to walk on mountains.

> *The list may end up being a million little things and big things I miss about you.*

Jesus Stream

A quiet, silent response. Selah

Journal Prompt

Can you rejoice today? If so, what will you rejoice about? How can you include prayer, song, or your unique creativity in your rejoicing? Make a determination and declaration to rejoice.

Day 69, March 27, 2020, Selah, quiet interlude

Day 70, March 28, 2020

Dear Jesus, Thank You for the quiet. The rest. The respite. Wayman is gone, he is not coming back. Oh, how I miss him. In the routines of morning. I am thankful. Green tea, my early morning drink. Quiet with You. Rest. Peace. Joy. Thankfulness.

"God, keep us near your mercy-fountain and bless us! And when you look down on us, may Your face beam with joy!"

Jesus Stream

A quiet Selah.

Journal Prompt

Have you found some rest? Can you move nearer to the mercy-fountain of God's love? Can you tell God how you see His banner of love over you? Can you find a slice of joy? Run to that joy.

Day 71, March 29, 2020

Dear Jesus, I love You. You are my strength and my power and my way. In You alone I put my praise.

Psalm 1:3 TPT

"...bearing fruit in every season of his life."

So, Lord, I just listened to You tell me about people. Words to encourage them. Thank you, Lord. I love You. Thank You. Lord, You set up my times and my appointments. May each be holy and powerful and magnify You, Jesus. You are so, so good. Thank You for being sure that in every season we will harvest. Thank You, Lord. Now You will bless my time. More than I can dream or imagine. This is so special. A holy perspective of time. I am so thankful.

Jesus Stream

Oh, Sara. Keep hanging out with me. I hold you. I breathe on you. You are NOT alone. I am with you. You are mine. My beloved. My beautiful one. My messenger of hope, faith, and joy. So, my dear one, keep listening. Keep being obedient. I will help you. It is like a time jump. (Judy Bennett is correct!) You will do more than you can dream or imagine. Because of Me. I am the Source, dear one. Your journal is My journal. Your podcast is My podcast. They are all really Mine. You offer, and people find Me through your words, your example. Your faith. Your joy. Your hope. Your insight.

I will never run out of creativity to pour on you. Forever. I know you miss Wayman so so so so much. You were one. Just as I had planned. Keep focusing on Me. You are My bride. Beautiful one. Strong one. Righteous one. Faithful one. I am so proud of you. You are My beautiful one. So today, just soak in Me. Releasing My love as never before. I hold you. I love you. This day is yours.

Love,

Jesus

Journal Prompt

What do you hear Jesus calling you? Ask Him for His special names for you. Ask Him to show you the fruit in your life. You are not barren, but full of fruit and more to come. Tell Jesus how He is your source of all that is good and beautiful.

Day 72, March 30, 2020

Oh, Jesus, I love You. I can hear You. You want people to know You. Yes, You! Now we can dive deep into my book study on Facebook using *Small Beginnings: A Journey to the Impossible.* It will help me with writing the companion journal as I do the book study with the online community.

What format? What video conferencing system? So many questions that I don't have the answers to yet. Oh Jesus, You are so good. Help me to schedule my day around Your will. I love You so much. It has been ten weeks now that Wayman has been gone. I am praising You. I am so thankful for the renewed purpose. A repurpose. A transition for me. The last fourteen days in Medina have been a respite. I am so thankful. So very thankful. O Jesus! Help me to let You flow through me.

"Let every activity of your lives and every word that comes from your lips be drenched with the beauty of our Lord Jesus, the Anointed One. And bring your constant praise to God the Father because of what Christ has done for you!"

Constant praise to You, God!

Jesus Stream

Oh, My daughter. You are My beloved. I love you. You do bring My fragrance to others. So dear one, keep on keeping on. Day by day. My love for you is pouring on and filling your pain of Wayman. It was his day to come home. Let me teach you even deeper about who I am. I am aware of it all. I bless you with the Small Beginnings Bible study online. Yes, day after day. You are My daughter. You have surrendered it all. I am with you in these days. Creating. Writing. Pouring out to My daughters in the online community you are building. I love you. Keep watching Me. Talk to Me. Sing to Me. I love you. I am accelerating you even more. Keep your eyes on Me. I love you, Sara.

Love,

Jesus Christ

Journal Prompt

What have you heard from Jesus today? Dear one, know He is speaking to your heart. I pray for open heavens for you to know you are hearing His voice. Write a prayer to Him about what you are hearing.

Day 73, March 31, 2020

Wow! What a wonderful blessing today was! Eating healthy. Writing a letter to my email list. God, You are so good. Thank You for guiding my ways. May I always keep my eyes on You. I love You, Jesus. Show me what to do. Jesus, I will praise you. You know my thoughts before I say them.

Psalms 139:1-2 TPT

"Lord, you know everything there is to know about me. You perceive every movement of my heart and soul, and you understand my every thought before it even enters my mind."

Jesus Stream

Oh dear, Sara. Yes, I Am the I Am. I know it all. I see it all. You being a widow does not surprise Me. I am proud of you counting every day as precious. Enjoying the husband I gave you. You did. Every minute of every day. I am so proud of you, Sara Lee Coston Thurman. So, now, work on your grief journey book and devotional. I will show you what to write. Yes, sooner than later. I am proud of you. Keep on keeping on. The sweetest of life. I am going before you. Everything you are concerned about — taxes, solar panels, hospital bills, and more. I am taking care of everything for you. Watch Me. Trust Me. Have faith in Me. You are My beautiful one. Oh, My dear. Yes, you are My beloved!

Love,

Jesus

> You are in charge of your own healing.

Journal Prompt

What are you most concerned about in your life right now? Can you turn it over to Jesus? He wants you to trust Him. His eyes are on you. He is not surprised by anything happening in your life.

Day 74, April 1, 2020, Selah, quiet interlude

Day 75, April 2, 2020

Dear Jesus, thank You for Your love. Jesus, I pray I can do this. My lower back is in pain. What is going on with the pain? Jesus, would You relieve this pressure? Jesus, come to me. Settle my spirit. Take away the pain. Help me to focus. My mind is going every which way. I can't read a book, except the Bible. I just want to worship You. I say to You — blessing and glory and wisdom and thanksgiving and honor and power and strength belong to our God, forever and ever. So, Lord, I praise You. All glory to You.

Revelation 7:12 NLT

"They sang, 'Amen! Blessing and glory and wisdom and thanksgiving and honor and power and strength belong to our God forever and ever! Amen.'"

Jesus Stream

Count on Me darling one. Rest in Me. I am your anchor. I am using you. Don't get distracted. Just focus on My timeline. I will, and am, showing favor to you. Step by step. Day by day. Yes, work on your grief journey devotional. Yes, work on your book about you and Wayman — 27,000 miles. Yes, get chapter one completed of your Prayer Journal for Small Beginnings. Take the next step. I am holding your hand. We are dancing. I am proud of you for your obedience in keeping the Bible study commitment twice a week.

I am giving you wisdom regarding decisions about your home. What loans to pay off and when. You will have different streams of income and more will be coming. Oh, my darling, come away with Me. Give Me the blessings. Glory. Wisdom. Thanksgiving and honor and power and strength, I love you, dear one. Let's do this. I am your everything. Hang with Me. I love you! I love you, Jesus.

Journal Prompt

Do you have physical pain showing up in your body in any place? Pray, and ask God the source of this pain and ask Him to lift it off, totally and completely. Jesus wants to show you His healing pathway to better health. Is there anything you need to be doing differently with your eating, exercise, or sleep patterns? Ask God to show you any changes you need to make. Begin worshiping God however you can, He will give you the strength to help you on your journey.

> *I know you are tired of being so sad. But be sad today because at some point 'tomorrow' you won't be as sad as you are today.*

Overview of Days 76 through 100

Feelings: Still deep sadness but feelings of purpose; dreaming of what God would have me do in this season is beginning to emerge with clarity.

I began to experience more peace in my spirit because I was releasing Wayman into God's plans of eternal life.

Thankfulness begins to emerge as a feeling every day for all we had together. The half empty glass was changing into the half full glass.

I begin to see the greater picture of eternity for Wayman, and for all followers of Christ, as the gift of eternal life to be the beautiful promise from God.

I began to have new trust in God to take care of me and every single need I had.

I was gaining clearer focus on what I was to do with my life on a daily routine in this season of grieving. I felt my brain fog lifting and clarity of mind. However, some days I was exhausted and unfocused, and my brain was foggy and not clear.

As I neared 100 days, intense waves of grief washed over me and kept me under water for hours it seemed. I did not know if I could come up for air. The pain was so deep and piercing.

What I needed during this season:

- An ear to listen to what I was feeling without trying to fix me.
- Permission to continue to grieve deeply.
- Patience. Do not try to rush me. I want to feel this pain of the great loss of My Man.

- Visitors. Drop by to see me. You can text first, if you want, or not. I am so very lonely. I would love to have you drop by.

- Grace for others in my family who were also grieving. Release my expectations of others behavior.

What I did not need during this season:

- Others telling me time would heal my pain.

- Others telling me year two would be easier than what I was going through today.

- People who thought I had cried enough already.

- To be ignored.

Day 76, April 3, 2020

Dear Jesus — You released Your message of love going deep within me this day. Thanks, Jesus, Holy Spirit, and Papa God.

Song of Songs 2:10 TPT

"My lover said to me, 'Rise up my darling! Come away with Me, My fair one!'"

Jesus, You are raising me up. You are using me. Lord, all I have is Yours. So, I thank You for helping me with my podcast, Small Beginnings with Sara. Thank You for placing this dream inside of me last month. It is coming to fruition. Show me when and how and where. Every detail is Yours, Jesus. You have gone before me. Download for me, Jesus. Oh, Jesus, I am Yours. Bless the works of my hands. Lord, I am excited to do the next steps with You.

Proverbs 31:13 TPT

"She searches out continually to possess that which is pure and righteous. She delights in the work of her hands."

Jesus Stream

Oh, My darling, you are rising up. I have taken you away with Me. Small Beginnings Journal. Small Beginnings podcast. So now I want you to paint with Me. Rest with Me. Rise up with Me. It is good. Well done on your video, your Bible Study this morning. I say even more, obedience is beautiful to Me. Come, My dear one. Rise up. My fair one.

Love,

Jesus

Journal Prompt

Ask God how to rest in Him, how to come away with Him. Do you feel any new purpose, renewed purpose in your life since your loss? Ask God to reveal to your heart what is pure and righteous. What work do you delight in with your hands? He will show you His plans.

Day 77, April 4, 2020

Dear Jesus, You are my delight. Lord, You are my one and only. Lord thank You for showing me the way of life. The narrow gate. The beautiful way. Thank You, Jesus, for rainy days.

Matthew 7:13 TPT

"The narrow gate and the difficult way leads to eternal life— so few even find it!"

Holy are You, Jesus. I love You. Help me to rest in You and also be super productive in this period of time. Bless me with the illuminated path. Thank You, Jesus.

Psalm 121:3-4 TPT

"He will guard and guide me, never letting me stumble or fall. God is my keeper; He will never forget nor ignore me. He

will never slumber or sleep; He is the Guardian - God for His
people, Israel."

Oh Lord, God Almighty. You are my King. My Rock.

Jesus Stream

Yes, I am. So now, Sara, My darling one. My beautiful one. My love. My precious light. Singing high on the hill. Come to Me. You are a beautiful warrior for me. Helping to bring My message of love to others. You are hearing Me. I am so proud of you for the online Bible study. It will bring many to know me better. Stay the path. I am your Guide. The podcasts will come quickly. The Small Beginnings Prayer Journal will come quickly. So daughter, I am lighting your path. Trust Me. Trust Me. I don't sleep. I am awake and preparing the way. I am going before you with every detail. Watch Me. Hear from Me. I love you and am releasing you to the world as light shining brightly — full of hope and joy for Me! Let's go dear one!

Journal Prompt

What has been the narrow gate for you today? Thinking about the promise of God never sleeping, how does this make you feel? Tell God how you need Him to not forget you in this season of life.

Day 78, April 5, 2020, Palm Sunday

Dear Jesus, thank You for coming. For Your obedience. For loving me well. For saving my life. For giving me eternal life. For saving Wayman and my kids and grandkids. Oh, Jesus, I love You! Help me today to be with You. To praise You. O Hosanna. My Yahweh. My Savior. My King. My Friend.

Jesus Stream

I know you miss Wayman. Your Man. Oh My dear one, I made you to love each other. I made you for each other. The ache is big. Deep. Bleeding hearts. Yes. Of course. I am God. The Great I AM. My darling, I love you with an everlasting love. It will never leave you. I am in your thoughts. In your processes. Today is a beautiful day. Celebrate my obedience. Let's rejoice for what I did that defeated death. Your man is with Me. I have a purpose for you, dear Sara. You are being obedient and releasing my love like an overflowing cup. Keep it up. So, let's do this. Full of joy and peace and love.

Journal Prompt

How have you been able to be obedient on this journey? Can you see how God is pleased with your obedience? Tell Him who He is to you. He defeated death on the cross.

Day 79, April 6, 2020

Thanks, Jesus for taking me deep today. Holy connections. Deeper pruning revealed to my heart. A generous heart connected to obedience. The online Bible study I am doing had sixty views today. Thanks, Jesus. Let Your truth settle on us. Use us all to be Your glory carriers. Hope carriers. Jesus, I love You. Your plans are beautiful.

Proverbs 3:6 NLT

"Seek His will in all you do and He will show you which path to take."

Lord, You will move mountains. You will make the path straight for me.

Jesus Stream

Oh, dear one. You are My darling. My beautiful one. Obedience is beautiful. I can count on My people. Generous giving brings great joy to My heart. Thank you for spreading the truth. For encouraging My children. Oh, Sara, good job! Well done! I love you. Watch as I make the way as you seek Me. In every step. Every place. Every space.

Journal Prompt

Do you have any sense of God showing you the path to take? Tell God what you are doing to seek His will. Believe He will show you the next steps. Are you spreading God's truth? If so, in what ways? If not, why not?

Day 80, April 7, 2020

Dear Jesus,

Thank You for giving me peace. Purpose. Your love and strength and joy flows through me Jesus. Thank You for your favor and blessings. I trust You. You alone. You are my strength. My Rock. My Peace. My Plans. The lover of my soul. My Savior. My Friend. So, Lord, help me with my first 100 days of my grief journey. How hard this journey is. Show me, Jesus, how to take the next step.

Hebrews 12:2 TPT

"We look away from the natural realm and we fasten our gaze onto Jesus who birthed faith within us and who leads us forward into faith's perfection."

Wow, Lord. You went to the cross so I can have joy. You sit at the right hand of the throne of God. Thanks, Jesus. Wow! Oh, Wow!

Jesus Stream

I AM the I AM. I am the perfector and finisher of your faith. Fasten your gaze on Me! So, trust Me, dear one. We have this. I am with you. I am God. I sit with Father God. I release angels to help you. I have joy for you. Your business is OK. Let's do this dear one. I am bringing out the gold in you. Trust Me.

Love,

Jesus

> *Don't ask if you do not have time to listen.*

Journal Prompt

Where is your faith needing new strength? Tell Jesus. How can you keep your gaze fastened on Jesus? How can you infuse vibrance and newness into your faith? How can you worship alone, now that you have lost your loved one? Can you do this with others as mentors, leaders, or spiritual pilgrims? If so, in what ways?

Day 81, April 8, 2020

Thank you for my purposes being brought forth. Help me to know You will open new doors for me, to understand what You want from me. My true help comes to my rescue.

Psalm 3:8 TPT

"For the Lord alone is my Savior. What a feast of favor and bliss He gives His people."

Jesus Stream

Dear one, you have this. I AM with you. You are My delight. I am your delight.

Journal Prompt

Ask Jesus for your purposes on earth. Ask Him to renew and repurpose your life. It is different and will never be the same. Jesus knows what He wants to reveal to you for this new season. Ask Him.

Day 82, April 9, 2020

Dear Jesus, thank You for clarity of mind. You told me what to do. Focus on cross paintings. And another angel. Positioning myself. Created to be a voice of life and light. A beautiful course. Plant the seeds in my heart.

Psalm 18:19-24 TPT

"His love broke open the way,

and he brought me into a beautiful, broad place.

He rescued me—because his delight is in me!

He rewarded me for doing what's right and staying pure.

I will follow his commands and

I'll not sin by ceasing to follow him, no matter what.

For I've kept my eyes focused on his righteous words,

and I've obeyed everything that he's told me to do.

I've been blameless before him and followed all his ways,

keeping my heart pure.

And so Yahweh has rewarded me according to my righteousness,

because I kept my heart clean before his eyes."

The Lord lives. He has led me to a safe place. Medina. Lord help me focus today to get much done. I am blessed by You, Lord Jesus.

Jesus Stream

Oh, My darling. You delight in Me. I delight in you. Come to Me, dear one and watch Me work. The unforced rhythms of My grace. I delight in you so much. Your podcast plans today. Yeah! Start writing the book, maybe titled — My First 100 Days of My Grief Journey. So darling, hang with Me. I will be your Helper in beautiful ways. Let's do this. Release. Incubate. And release.

Journal Prompt

Ask Jesus for clarity of mind on specific needs you have. Any major decisions coming up? Jesus will give you His wisdom freely and help you focus on the important issues today.

Day 83, April 10, 2020, Good Friday

Oh Jesus — Thank You. We are overwhelmed with Your love. With Your joy. Thanks for helping me teach about self-control this morning. Lord, You know it all. You are my gift of life. Thanks for Wayman. I am so thankful. I am so blessed I was married to this man for nearly thirty-five years. Continue to teach me. Show me. Create in me a new heart. A fresh awakening of this season and this time to hear You. You bless me so much.

Oh Lord, eighty-three days have passed since I touched My Man. How I miss him. Thanks for being my deep comfort. Providing for me. My every need. Repurposing me for being able to shine for You. All glory to You, King Jesus. To the cross You went. Thanks. Death is defeated. Eternal life is mine. It is Wayman's already. Thank You, Jesus.

Song of Songs 2:10 TPT

"...For now is the time, My beautiful one."

Jesus Stream

Come away with Me. Yes, My darling, My beautiful one. You are pointing the way to others. To be the cup overflowing. To be healed and then overflow to others. Oh, Sara, My beautiful one. Keep crying. Thanks for releasing self-control. Discipline. Perseverance. To get to the bigger harvest. It takes hard work. Focus. You are doing it. I am so proud of you. Yes, My darling. Watch. I am sending you helpers. All along the way.

Love, Jesus

Journal Prompt

Can you grasp the gift of eternal life for your loved one? Truly it is the greatest gift to be given by God. Death is defeated. Can you write a thank You letter to God for this gift to you and your loved one?

Day 84, April 11, 2020, Selah, quiet interlude

Day 85, April 12, 2020, Easter Sunday

Dear Jesus. Thank You. King. Savior. Friend. I am so thankful for You. For eternal connection. Never to be left alone. Or forgotten. Only You, Jesus. I am thankful. I miss Wayman Lee Thurman more than I ever thought possible. Your comfort is real. Thanks for bringing me to Medina to be with Justin, Ana, and Lilian so I can feel relief from my deep grief, my bleeding heart. I am so thankful how this space and place is comforting to me. Lord, my eyes are on You. Fixed on You. Not moving. Always there. Always here. Eternity.

Jesus Stream

Oh, My darling, Sara. Yes. Everything is being made new. I Am the I Am. Nothing passes through Me that I don't approve of or allow. So, trust Me, Sara Lee Thurman. I bring the wind. I bring the rain. I bring the sun. I bring the new. I treasure the old. Your story. Stay with Me. Keep your eyes on Me. I will not let you down. I am with you, Sara Lee Coston Thurman, for all eternity. I have your man. He is home with Me. Safe and not separated by Me or from Me. He is with Me. He is My joy forever. I went to the cross for him, for Wayman, so he could be with Me forever. So, I can see it all. You are My story. Keep letting Me write your script. I love you today and tomorrow. Forever and always.

Journal Prompt

What is your view of eternity? Can you ask God for a deeper understanding of His plans? How has God sent helpers along the way to you? Can you count them as gifts from God?

> *Keep your eyes on God, He will not let you down.*

Eternity

by Sara Thurman

Today and tomorrow
Forever and always
In this place
In this space
My Jesus
You are my friend
My Savior
You are my Hope
My Comfort
You are my Eternity
My Faithful One
You open up the balconies of heaven
You make everything new
My Man is home with You
Today and tomorrow
Forever and always
You are my Eternity, too.

Easter Sunday, April 12, 2020, Day 85

I wrote this about living without My Man. I was asking God for understanding of His plans for eternity.

Day 86, April 13, 2020

Oh, Lord — I am so thankful. The butterflies flutter. The butterflies come. They are Yours. I am Yours. Thankful for bringing out my need to have forgiveness of others. You are the repairer of the ancient walls.

Amos 9:10 NLT

"On that day I will restore the fallen house of David. I will repair its damaged walls. From the ruins I will rebuild it and restore its former glory."

Jesus Stream

Yes, you must forgive others to have the "more" I want to give to you. I am sending messages along your path. You are starting to make moves toward restoration.

Journal Prompt

Can you see anything new coming into your life? Tell God about the new places He is building to restore what has been lost. Ask Him for more.

Day 87, April 14, 2020, Selah, quiet interlude

Day 88, April 15, 2020

Dear Jesus, settle my heart to yours. Help me focus and use this day for your glory. All of you, dear Jesus. Not my will, but Yours. Help me to write the two letters. To work on the podcast. Thank You for helping me focus. I say, "give me focus." It is so hard to think. To remember what to do. It is exhausting unless You are helping me. Clarity of mind. Purpose in all I do. Lord, let my purpose come forth today. Oh, I love You, Lord. Help me to hear You.

Jesus Stream

Oh, My daughter, My darling. My sweetest Sara. Just come and rest with me. Watch Me. I will take care of everything for you. You are Mine. I am your Defender. In all areas. So, my darling, hang with Me. I am moving. Mightily. For you. For Me. Helping others. Believe what only I can do. I am using you. So, join in with me. Writing cards to those I tell you to. Listening and being obedient to My instructions. Oh, Sara, you are mine. Podcast coming to life in a few weeks. Small Beginnings Prayer Journal coming to life this year. Paintings are selling. You have money to pay your taxes. Paying off the car debt. Rearranging your other debt to be reduced quickly. The Lord is who I Am. I will show you how to do all of this. Grief journey. It is not easy. It is hard. Your first 100 days. Yes, My darling. Let's do this. I will complete the work I have begun!

Acts 20:24 NLT

"But my life is worth nothing to me unless I use it for finishing the work assigned to me by the Lord Jesus — the work of telling others the Good News about the wonderful grace of God."

Journal Prompt

How are you doing with tasks? With the "to do list?" Ask God for focus and clarity of mind to rest in His timing and direction and to help in times of need.

Day 89, April 16, 2020

Dear Jesus, thanks for today. I rested well. Thanks so much, Jesus. I love You. You are my King. My Savior. My Friend. Lord, You are to lead me. Today — You helped me with the podcast. You helped me name my new art pieces. Lord, show me. Teach me. I love You. Jesus. Thank You for giving me the money to pay Wayman's hospital bill. To pay other bills. Favor was given to me with a discount for one bill. There is more. I can worry about them. But I am choosing to trust You. You are the Door Opener. Trusting You, Jesus. Show me how to make the most out of this today. Lord, show me the next steps. I am so thankful for ALL You are doing. Help me to stay in my lane. To trust You. To love those around me. To love You. To love myself. You are my Rock. My Friend.

I Timothy 6:17, 21 TPT

"Trust instead in the one who lavishes upon us all good things, fulfilling our every need...May God's grace empower you always!"

Jesus Stream

Oh, daughter, slow down. You have done a lot. Let Me lead you. Guide you. Be your REST. I love you so much. I AM the Great I AM. I ask that you do

81

TRUST Me — I lavish upon you all good things — fulfilling your every need. Thanks — Yes — Keep your eyes on Me. I have the pathway of righteousness. Faithfulness. Keep your eyes fixed on Me. Guard every thought. My grace pours over you. Focus on blessings this day.

Journal Prompt

Write a list of blessings God has done for you since your loss. Can you see how He is making the way for you? Tell Him your needs and watch Him take care of you by lavishing good things on you. This is His promise. Receive His grace.

Day 90, April 17, 2020

Dear Jesus, thank You for wrapping me in the shadows of Your wings. A safe and holy place. Help me to keep my eyes on You. Every day. Every minute. To walk out on the water. Day after day. To do what You have placed in front of me. The on-line Bible study with *Small Beginnings: A Journey to the Impossible* has been full of purposes I did not realize.

How blessed I am to follow You. When we take a step, You always show up. You are there. You are here.

Jesus Stream

Oh, daughter, you are My darling daughter. Hang out with Me and I will never leave you. Let's do this. This work in front of you is for Me. Podcast. Bible Study. Paintings.

Journal Prompt

Write about your next step. It may be sitting and waiting. Or it may be a new action. Tell Jesus about your next step.

Day 91, April 18, 2020

Dear Jesus — it is my birthday. You knew before the beginning of time You would have me be born sixty-two years ago today. The youngest daughter of Hugh and Olga Coston. Thanks, Jesus, for who You made me to be. Thanks for flowing through me. Ministering to my soul, dear Jesus. I am listening to United Pursuit, singing praises to You in the Spirit.

Lord, I ask You to tell me more of Your mysteries. Lord, You say, "Ask!" So, I am asking You to tell me what You want to tell me. Do so, Lord. I am listening. I am waiting. I am Yours. Tell me what You want.

My goals this year at age 62:

- I want to live each day to the fullest for You, to bring glory to Your name in all I do, say, create, and write.

- I want to bring honor to my life with Wayman Lee Thurman. I didn't want to be widowed at age 61. But I was and today I am 62. Lord, help me to lead others to know Your joy in the beautiful marriage covenant.

- I want to have more tools to help others. E-courses on creativity, hearing God's voice, bible studies, grief book, the first 100 days on what to say, to do or not do. The 27,000 Miles book on our marriage. The Small Beginnings Prayer Journal. The podcast — Small Beginnings with Sara. And art — Lord — whatever, You tell me.

Thanks for leading me. Guiding me. Inspiring me. So, Lord this year is Yours. Thanks for giving me so much. My heart is full, but I am in a void because Wayman has gone home to You. How I miss him. I know You know how much I love him. And I can go on. Thanks, Jesus, for my family. I am blessed.

Jesus Stream

My daughter. My darling. You have no idea. You are My beautiful one. Oh, My daughter. I have so much for you. Keep your eyes and heart and soul fixed on me. You can count on Me. I am your strength. Your vision. 'Til the whole world knows Me. Thanks, dear one, for being obedient. You are My delight. I go before you and lead the way. Many will follow you. You are doing so well. Keep on dear one with your feelings. Your pain. Your loss. Rest in Me. I have your man. He is with me. Safe and secure. His marathon is over. Now My joy is complete. You will be reunited. So now for this moment you are sixty-two years old today. Rest in Me. I am holding you. I will never let you go. I am teaching you how to dance with Me. I love you, My darling daughter.

Love,

Jesus

Journal Prompt

Have you had a marker in time that has been difficult to enjoy because your loved one is not here? Tell Jesus about your experience.

Day 92, April 19, 2020

Dear Jesus, I am sixty-two years old now. Ok, that is good. Not bad. Help me to count my body as Yours. Keep it healthy and full of life and energy. Grieving is hard. Thanks, Jesus! I ask for Your help today in reading and writing and my walks. It is hard for me to concentrate or focus for very long. I am prepping for Bible study. I need help with solutions for my finances. Make it easy Lord. You know the steps I need to take. Show me. Teach me. Let me listen to You. My eyes are on You, not on man. Thanks, Jesus. I will look up to the mountains and the hills longing for help. But then I realize that our true help and protection comes only from the Lord.

"I look up to the mountains—does my help come from there? My help comes from the Lord, who made the heavens and the earth!"

Jesus Stream

Sara, you must stay close to Me, Hang out with Me, morning, noon, and night. I Am the great I Am. You must keep your eyes on Me. Watch Me. I have you. Your plans are My plans. Step by step, Small Beginnings. Yes, My daughter. We can do this. I am using you to bring forth My love message of hope and glory and true transformation of heart connection with others. So, let's do this. Bless you, sweet daughter. Oh yes! We love this. Listen to Me. I love you. I am proud of you. I am your shield and protector.

Isaiah 26:2-3 NLT

"Open the gates to all who are righteous: all the faithful to enter. You will keep in perfect peace all who trust in You, all whose thoughts are fixed on you!"

> *You are in perfect peace if your mind is on Me.*

Love,

Jesus

Journal Prompt

What are your rhythms of spending time with Jesus? Talk to Him about what you need for peace.

Day 93, April 20, 2020

Dear Jesus — Thanks for an amazing Bible study with You today. You came. You always do and bring revelation and peace.

Jesus Stream

Quiet Selah

Journal Prompt

What results have you had lately from reading your Bible? What passages are speaking into your life?

Day 94, April 21, 2020

Dear Jesus, I was interrupted yesterday. Today my thoughts are considering Your purposes for me. I am feeling new connections with people in the online Bible study. I am being used by You to inspire and encourage others with my own personal story and examples. Thank You, Lord, for using me. For helping me find Your purposes in my life. I am so thankful, Jesus. You are my Guide. My Comfort. My Purpose for living. My Grace. My Lover. My Dream-Maker. My Heart-Song. My Creator. My Rock. My Embracer. My Defender. My Protector. My Lover of My Soul. My Beautiful One. My King. My God. My Savior. My Friend. This is who You are. The Great I AM! I put my trust in You. My Light. And I am a child of the light.

John 12:36 TPT
"So believe and cling to the light while I am with you, so that you will become children of light."

Jesus Stream

Oh, My darling Sara. You are my little light. Shining bright for Me in your grief and anguish. Your Wayman. Your "My Man" is so very pleased with you. Keep going with a purpose for Me — to make My name famous all over the world. Yes, and amen, daughter. Clarity on the purposes and tasks in front of you. I am with you. I am your Guide and Defender and Friend.

Journal Prompt

Write the names of God that were meaningful to you today. Call on Him in personal ways and ask for what you need. He is your promise keeper.

Day 95, April 22, 2020

I can't breathe again. The pain is so great. He is not coming back home. I am here with the kids. But when I go home, you won't be there, Wayman Lee Thurman. It is just me. Half my heart is gone.

Dear Jesus, thank You for making all things possible. You have given me all I need. Step by step. Not too fast - just day by day. Step by step. Thanks. Today, writing my grief journey book, thinking of podcast ideas, and even more exercise. I keep learning. Thank You, Jesus, for new mercies every day!

Jesus Stream

Yes, look at Me and your face will glisten with My glory. Join your life with Mine and joy will come. No more shame. Let's do this, My darling. We have this. Joy is here. Focus. There is so much more even though I know you can't see it. You have this, My darling! I love you, Sara Lee Coston Thurman. You are mine!

Love,

Jesus

Journal Prompt

It seems like the pain will never end. Write and tell God about this deep and seemingly never-ending pain. He wants to hear your heart.

Day 96, April 23, 2020

We are getting close to 100 days without you, Wayman. It seems like 100 years of separation, not 100 days. Three months and ten days used to be shorter to me. But not now. 100 days seems like forever. How I want to understand eternity even more. A slice of time without you. But this slice is so heavy and thick. It seems too much to bear. You are waiting for me on the other side.

Dear Jesus, Show me Your passion, Your love. What is my purpose? I need to know to keep going. This is so hard. My connection with You to create from there, that place?

Thank You, Lord, for giving me Your passion of love. Thanks for giving me space and time to be with You. Nothing else matters but You, Jesus. Please help me Jesus to know what to do. To put my hands to Your plow. I will do it, Jesus. You are so good. You are my Helper. My Guide. My Creator. So, Lord, teach me. Clean me. Purify my thoughts. Put a shield around me where I am protected. Lord--You are my Defender. My Provider. Lord, I surrender to You. Show me. Teach me. Guide me. This book in front of me to write, the journal for Small Beginnings. Help me get this completed in the next two weeks, if not sooner. And Lord, help me with *The First 100 Days: My Grief Journey of Losing My Man.*

(Note: the working title changed many times during the writing process of more than a year.)

Today is day ninety-six. So hard. But You God have been my solace. So, now Lord, let me hear from You.

My prayer today from

Genesis 26:12 NLT:

"When Isaac planted his crops that year, he harvested a hundred times more grains than he planted, for the LORD blessed him."

100-Fold. Yes, Lord. 100 book sales. 100 e-course sales. Yes, Lord. Thank You!

> *You are my hope, my comfort, my love, my eternity.*

Jesus Stream

So, My daughter, keep planting new seeds. Pinterest. IG stories, oh, Sara, do it. You can. Drive the reader to a link to purchase what you have planted. Keep listening to me. I am the King; I am the One! Let's do this dear one. Bless you today! I am your Guide. Keep moving forward. Sara Lee Thurman--I will bring you favor and provision. I love you. I have your grieving heart!

Journal Prompt

How has the time changed for you? Has time sped up or slowed down? Talk to God about time and eternity.

Day 97, April 24, 2020, Selah, quiet interlude

Day 98, April 25, 2020

Late morning reflections.

Dear Jesus, I have been talking to you all morning. But just now writing my words down. Day ninety-eight without My Man. How can I keep going? This road is so hard. I feel like it has been ninety-eight years since Wayman has been gone from my side. My bed. Our hand in hand walks.

Words To Wayman on Day 98: I miss your morning smiles. I miss fixing your green tea and bringing it to your bedside. Oh, how you served me all those years. Coffee, lunches packed, breakfast to go in the car, and then dinner ready when I got home late. I think you changed more diapers than I did on our son's bottoms. I was in grad school and working as a middle school teacher full-time. You were working a full-time job, too. But you were there. Serving. Loving me, the boys, all the time.

I am journaling these words, but they really do not tell about my heart. How can I use words to describe my pain? My ache? My bleeding heart? I miss your touch. You walk by me, just a gentle pat on the arm or on my back. In the mornings, when I was brushing my teeth or my hair, a gentle touch on my back, or even my bottom. Our hugs when we departed. Our kisses every morning and every night. I could go on and on about what I miss about you. But your gentle touch is a void. A place I miss so much. Oh, so much. It is gone. I have the memories. I have the love you gave me, day after day. But I miss you, Wayman Lee Thurman! My Man. My lover. My husband. Three weeks short of thirty-five years of loving you. I knew on our first date I was going to marry you. You made me feel loved and special. I felt adored by you. You made me a better person for thirty-five years. Then, I wrote the rough draft of all I shall become.

Reflections later in the day.

I walked to the creek. Wallace Creek, to reflect. Looking for solace. Looking for answers to this deep groaning loneliness. I found peace in the sound of the creek. I dropped a single yellow wildflower in the water and watched it go out of sight. I cried. Like My Man, the flower is gone.

This day is hard. One of my hardest so far. It seems like Wayman has been gone for ninety-eight years. I pulled away from my kids and packed a picnic lunch and walked a few miles to the creek. I never stopped praying. God, why? If love like this love you gave me for thirty-four years and forty-nine weeks was so wonderful, why would you take it away? Why would this perfect holy matrimony end with the death of Wayman, My Man, my husband? I don't understand how life is described by You as a fleeting moment, like a vapor. My Man is gone from this earth, and he is not coming back.

Oh, the pain of not having his touch. I know we experience Jesus with our five senses. Taste, touch, seeing, hearing, and smelling. I experienced Wayman's love through the five senses. And on this day, I miss his touch. My tears flow thinking I will never have him hold my hand again. Pat my shoulder as he walked by. Touch my face. Kiss my mouth. Dry my back in the place I never could reach with my towel after my bath. His touch was gentle and sweet, always portraying his love for me. Never harsh or in anger. I am blessed that these are my memories.

Words to Wayman: Oh, Wayman Lee, I miss your touch. The way it told me that you cherished me. You adored me. I was your wife. You steadied me by your touch. You anchored me by your touch. You guided me by your touch. You communicated to me by your touch. It is a void. A hole. A darkness. But when I think of your touch, I am thankful to have had such a strong man love me like you loved me. I knew your love by your touch. And I miss your touch so very much. No words can describe the emptiness I feel deep in my soul. I can't replace you, Wayman. I miss you more than I ever knew I would. More than I could imagine. Will my pain subside? It doesn't feel like it ever will. I am in the throes of deep soul wrenching pain from your absence. My tears come like waves crashing down my face. I cry out to God for comfort. I find rest in a hot bath. And I paint. I worship my King. I paint the still waters I sat by. I paint the yellow flower I watched flow down the creek. My tears dried for a few hours, and they came again. Ninety-eight days without you. It seems like ninety-eight years I have been grieving. Will my grieving ever end?

Jesus Stream

My Sara, dearest darling. You are doing so well. I will tell you when you don't say something to honor Wayman. Yes, what you two had! My gift to you both was beautiful and perfect and holy. I want you to share. To let people know of the beautiful oneness that is there for them. I designed it that way. I am the perfect Creator. I am proud of you for taking notes already and being in the process of writing your book about your marriage with Wayman, 27,000 Miles. I was in the middle of your lives. I want your testimony shared. Oh, Sara, My dearest, I love you. You are doing well. I have provided another safe place for you to heal, create, and write, at the lake with Roland and Ann.

Psalm 72:17 TPT

"So that His name may be honored forever! May the fame of His name spring forth! May it shine on, like the sunshine! In Him all will be blessed to bless others, and may all the people bless the One who blessed them."

Journal Prompt

Are the waves of pain continuing to crash upon you? Ride it out. The pain is real. Don't try to lessen the pain, just let it cover you. God is with you. Can you write to Him about what you are experiencing? He already knows and is with you.

Day 99, April 26, 2020

Morning reflections:

Dear Jesus. Today is day ninety-nine. Do You know my pain? I drink my green tea by myself. I know You are here. But Wayman is not. How can I go on? This is really, really, really hard. Did You have to take him when You did? I miss him so much. I can't even breathe. But Lord, how much harder can it get? I really don't know if I can make it. I just want Wayman back. This is the hardest journey; I did not think it would be THIS hard. Fourteen weeks today. Never to feel your touch again, Wayman. Never to have you look at me with such a cherished love.

Wayman is gone. I am so sad, Lord. Help me. Restore my broken heart. I don't even know how to move forward. But step by step. Day by day. With a thankful heart. Lots of tears. Lord, come to me. Be my strength. My hope. So, Lord, count my tears. Embrace me. Did I say how much I miss Wayman's touch? His hugs? His embrace? So, hold me, Jesus.

Jesus Stream

Oh, My beautiful one. My darling, Sara. I am with you in this grief. Day ninety-nine, I know. It is big. It is overwhelming, this grief you feel. It is in My plans. You have to trust Me. I know it all. I gave you My very best. I have not left you, My Sara. Let me lead you to the peaceful streams. I am with you, My darling. So, hang with Me. I love you. I catch your tears.

Love, Jesus

> Experience Jesus with all of your five senses.

Journal reflections later on Day 99:

I woke up crying. I cried all day until about thirty minutes before I went to sleep. One of my saddest days. A grief I could not slay. A grief that I just accepted and stayed in for hours upon hours. I laid on the floor of the gym and cried deeply for at least an hour. An hour of deep groans. The sound of a widow grieving the passing of her man. My tears knew no end today. I exercised hard at the gym, hoping to find relief from the sadness of my bleeding heart. To no avail. I laid on the floor and wept and groaned and cried so much. Anyone walking by would have called for help. The kind of deep groans I made when I was in labor. A pain so deep and guttural, it is not often a human makes these sounds. Here it is day ninety-nine and my grief is deeper than ever. I even thought, I am finished with this life. I cannot keep living. I am ready to join My Man. It is ok, everyone will be ok if I go now. I hate to even write this in my grief journey. It is a scary, yucky truth that gets all the healthcare professionals' attention. And that is ok. I told my friend Mary Lou. I told my son and daughter-in-law. They all felt I was safe. I did speak it. My deep, deep grief. At times, I could not breathe. I was physically overwhelmed with such sadness.

Journal Prompt

You have made it ninety-nine days. I am so proud of you. Minute by minute. Hour by hour. Day by day. You are doing it. One step at a time. Can you write a prayer of thanksgiving to Jesus for helping you get this far when you didn't know if you could make it past day four?

Day 100, April 27, 2020

What I wrote to a friend today —

Also, my heart is way better today. Deep grief and sadness have subsided substantially. For that, I am thankful. I believe God's strength came in and took over my weakness. Today is day 100 and I am making it.

Dear Jesus,

Thank You. I have made it to 100 days without My Man. Oh, God. I can make it. Days ninety-eight and ninety-nine were some of my most difficult days. It was so dark. It was lonely. I was not sure I could make it or would want to make it another day. I did reach out and share my deep, deep pain and asked for prayer for my intense grief. It was so deep I could not breathe. I needed help. I needed My Man.

But You, Jesus, became my strength when I had none left. You breathed on me. I am not sure how or why. But You did. You lifted my head another day. And you will again another day, and another. I am not done — even though I feel lonely. You gave me an encounter with You on the floor of the gym where I was working out. I was the only one in the gym at this time. I saw red, as I do when the Holy Spirit's presence is so thick. My eyes were closed, and tears were drenching my hair. My groans were deep and heavy. I no longer tried to keep them inside of me. I let them out. Loud and long wails to You, my God. And You came again with bright, bright red — like flowers that encompassed my vision of Your presence. I have never had a vision like this. Undeniably, Your hand of comfort told me You were near.

Thank You, Jesus. Today, Day 100, I awoke with hope and energy. I thought I would need to cancel my online Bible study with my girls, but I was ok. I could breathe. I could talk. I could hold onto Your strength. It came from You today, God. I was able to do some errands. I went on a walk. I identified two painted bunting birds with my phone app by the creek. God, You are so faithful. Use me.

100 days without My Man. A journey I wish no one would have to walk. Day by day. Walks. Talks. Hot baths. Green tea. Phone calls. Large prayers and then more prayers. An outpouring of love. My Defender, going before me. Holding me strongly in Your right hand. Collecting my tears. Touching my heart with the Holy Spirit. The presence of Jesus with visions of red I have never seen before.

Wayman Lee Thurman, I miss you more than I ever thought possible. And even more than that. I have to believe you are home. Jesus is blessed

94

to have you. We miss you. We miss you. We miss you and we miss you some more. How can I keep going without you?

Such a wave of grief comes to take my breath away. And I can't breathe, and I don't want to breathe. And then, I do breathe, and You allow my tears of deep grief to roll down my cheeks to my shirt or ears — depending on whether I am standing up or lying down. Tears in my ears from crying over you. A truth. Wayman would sing me a country song years ago that is now coming true. When you cry lying down, your tears do run into your ears. I know that for sure from first-hand experience.

So, 100 days. It is far from over this grief I am experiencing. This loss I never knew would be so, so hard. But today is a marker. 100 days. I have made it this far. The road is long and difficult. But God, You are with me. I miss his voice. I miss his laughter. I miss his kisses. I miss his touch. I miss his jokes and his stories. I miss his eyes, the way he looked at me. I miss his smell. His pillow has been washed. His fragrance is gone. I miss his singing. I miss his conversation. I miss his prayers. I miss his love, his never-ending and unfailing love. I miss his hands. I miss his face. I miss his smile. I miss his love.

I just keep writing and writing to You God on this 100th day since Wayman passed. Thank You for holding me in Your strong right hand. Thank You for crying with me. Thanks for loving me right where I am. Thank You, Jesus. There is no one like You. You are my comfort. My strength. My love. My purpose. When I think of you, I know You have poured into me Your love and Your desire so it can flow out to others. So, Lord, guide me. Be my strength. My joy. My purpose. My life. April is nearly over. Help me to focus and produce all You want me to produce. The Small Beginnings podcast. Lord, help me! Guide me. All the pieces are coming together. A membership site. Lord, I am yours. If I sit and praise You and pray, You are pleased. If I reach out with the tent stakes, You are pleased. You are my Guide. Lord, I only want to be in alignment with You. I sit with You and listen to Your guidance, Jesus. I lay it all down unless it is from You.

Journal Prompt

Who can you call when you need help? Make a list of treasured friends and family who will come to your aide. Tell them ahead of time that if you need them you will call. Do you need to seek professional help along your journey of grief? Do not be afraid or embarrassed to ask for help. Will you make this promise to yourself?

Open My Eyes

By Sara Thurman

I know that I know that I know that You help me
every day and every second to open my eyes.

In the middle of the night when I open my eyes,
I see Your assigned angels.

Open my eyes to see the burnt orange sunflower blooms.

My Faithful One

By Sara Thurman

You open up the balconies of heaven
You make everything new

My Man is home with You
Today and tomorrow
Forever and always

You are my Eternity, too

My Thoughts on the Next 100 Days

Lord, I want to think the next 100 days will be easier. But I don't know. I have You. Your promise to be with me forever. Never leaving me. So, I trust You. For the next 100 days, and the next 100 days after that. Into eternity. My Man's legacy lives on. A steady and sure force of strength yet gentleness. That was My Man. Goodbye, my honey. My husband. My friend. My companion. My anchor. My strength. My balance. My realignment. My wisdom. My back rubber. My Man. I love you forever, Wayman Lee Thurman.

Jesus Stream

Oh, Sara. I AM the I AM. I do see it all. Trust Me. I am your provision. Your light. Your lover. Your husband. Your protector. Your guide. I will show you the next steps. You have Me. I will guide you. I can see it all. I know your future. Trust Me. Today, My glory is your rear guard. I have gone before you and behind you. Keep in line with Me. Keep loving Me and fixing your eyes on Me. Keep taking people deeper with Me. I love you. Yes, I made painted buntings just for your joy. My very presence comes to you. Rest in Me. I am in charge. Listen. Watch. Increase your awareness. I love you so. I am so proud of you for leaning on Me. Keep close dear one. I am not going anywhere. I am proud of your rhythms of life. Of my grace and of my purposes for you. So, trust Me, dear one. Lean into Me. I am with you always and forever. No separation from you ever. Eternity is ours.

Journal Prompt

Let Jesus whisper to your heart. May you hear your renewed purposes. Write what you are thankful for on day 100. You have made it this far. God is so very pleased with your strength and perseverance.

Wayman's Bells

By Sara Thurman

I crave hearing your voice. Your laughter. Your snores. Your special sounds I grew to love and count on for comfort.

Christmas is coming. You are not here. Is there anything to help my empty heart?

On my daily walks I hear and see wind chimes. Like the rich sound of church bells in our neighborhood.

The bells. The wind chimes. We had some that sang in the wind with high notes. But I wanted the deep rich sounds as the wind moved through the trees like a breath of the Holy Spirit. A reminder of you.

Backordered. Will not arrive before Christmas. Did I want to adjust my order to another set? No, I will wait.

The bells arrived a day before and a year after your heart attack that changed everything. Jake hung them in the cedar tree in the backyard. You can hear them in your workshop. I can hear them in my art studio.

As I am writing this, I hear them singing and ringing deeply, reminding me of you. They resonate our love in my soul . They sing of our trust and oneness.

I call them Wayman's Bells. I can hear your laughter and feel your love. Eternity has not taken away but added to the sounds of our love.

February 14, 2021

Written after reflecting on the one-year anniversary of Wayman's death.

Living Beyond the First 100 Days

Practices to Help Your Heart Heal Along the Journey

 Is there something, someplace or a time that will help you anchor your memories to your loved one? Surprises may come up and you will know it is meant to be. For example, (this actually happened one year after Wayman's passing) I knew I needed a reminder of Wayman in the backyard. Something fresh and new. The sixty-five-inch Corinthian Bells were the perfect Christmas gift to myself. They did not arrive until the one-year anniversary of his death. The company even named their company after I Corinthians 13, the love chapter in the Bible. Now every time I walk in my backyard, I am aware of these bells, now called "Wayman's Bells." They bring me great comfort. If the breeze is not blowing, I often walk over and have them sing to me by moving the center paddle. These bells are an anchor of comfort to my heart.

 Write. Write. And write some more. Journal. Make poetry. Sit in their favorite seat. Write from their perspective. Remember. Allow yourself the place and the space to grieve. And write. Some medical research shows regular journaling after losing a loved one can help boost immune function as well as mood and well-being of the person grieving. I have included many of my poems and prose in this book as a way to reflect and find more meaning in grief. The process of writing with some loose structure has been healing for me and allowed me to connect words to my pain.

 Let the tears roll freely. Tears are a beautiful gift from God. More beautiful than I ever knew they were. Truly, God knew what He was doing when He created us with tear ducts and an unlimited supply of tears. Cry. Cry. And cry some more. Every single time you feel them coming, let them come.

 Feel your emotions that come up like a roller coaster off the track. Don't try to push them away. Feel all the feels. If it is anger, tell your deceased loved one how angry you are in the present circumstance. If it is intense sadness, sit with the sadness. Do not push it away. Ride it out like in an intense hurricane with the most intense winds ripping off your roof. Your emotions need to be released as they come up. I have learned that if I don't go with the emotion because I am so tired of being "sad" or "mad," it will rise again, even more intensely. Again, I repeat — feel all the feels. To get to the other side, or even closer to the middle, this process of experiencing your current emotions is a huge part of healing.

 Walk. Walk. And walk some more. Every day. I love what C.S. Lewis said about walking in *A Grief Observed*. "I do all the walking I can, for I'd be a fool to go to bed not tired." Maybe not on the same pathway you walked together with your loved one. I found a new route. I walk it every day or several times a day. Our regular route was too painful. I could not do it, unless it was with family when they came to visit. But recently, I took our route in the snow. It was the most beautiful walk. I could imagine My Man with me. It felt like he was watching and enjoying it right along with me. Fresh snow. An untouched path. Birds. A whitetail buck and doe. Snow on the trees. The quiet. The gentle breeze. Then the stillness. The clean and pure beauty of freshly fallen snow. Nearly ten inches, which is once every 100 years here in Central Texas. And this walk caused many tears to flow. Beautiful drops of sorrow released from my soul. Collected by Jesus. Purity and peace were present.

 Have a simple daily schedule to follow. Sleep patterns, eating well, and regular exercise are important for healing and oh so very difficult to do on a daily basis. Plan some simple meals to have on hand. Meals are so hard as we are eating alone now. Try to eat a healthy diet as the stressors of grieving take an extra toll on the body. Try to go to bed at a normal time. This is still very difficult for me. I hate going to bed alone. Increase personal exercise to the point of actually sweating. I find this extremely helpful to release toxins from the body as well as the tear ducts. After exercise I feel remarkably better and can make the harder phone calls and do the tasks I have dreaded. I restarted my twice weekly exercise routine with my personal trainer within two weeks after Wayman passed. I have continued this schedule and have actually added an additional day per week.

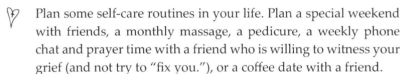 Plan some self-care routines in your life. Plan a special weekend with friends, a monthly massage, a pedicure, a weekly phone chat and prayer time with a friend who is willing to witness your grief (and not try to "fix you."), or a coffee date with a friend.

Epsom salt baths get a special paragraph. Seriously, I do not know what I would have done without Epsom salt baths daily, many days four and five times per day. I would light a few candles, get into my bathtub with plenty of fragrant Epsom salts and hot water, and sit. This is the place where I could cry and let my emotions flow. This was my safe place to process my grief. To cry and sob and cry some more. When my grief was overwhelming, I ran a hot bath and put in my favorite salts and soaked and cried and groaned until the water cooled. Or I ran more hot water in the tub and continued my journey of grief.

Create every day you are able. I have been a practicing artist since 2014 and selling my paintings since 2016. I believe God created each of us to be creative and as we spend time creating, we actually are spending time with God. I painted more than one hundred paintings in the first year after Wayman passed away. Have your creative area set up and ready to go with easy access. Go and sit and play with drawing, watercolor, acrylic, oil, or a combination of creative mediums. Sign up for an online art class or look at the thousands of free YouTube art lessons. Don't have any expectations of creating a masterpiece for yourself. There is a phenomenon called "creative flow" which allows the brain to rest. Has this ever happened to you when you lost track of time or forgot you were hungry while creating? Creating can be a restorative process in the midst of grief. Listen to God as you create. Enjoy the process. You will hear Him in the creative process. He will use your creative time to help restore your soul.

- Plant a garden or get new houseplants to care for that make your space beautiful. Even a few herbs in some pots at your kitchen window can help you by seeing a living object that needs you.

- Get a dog. But get a really good dog. A cute dog. A dog that will be your companion for walks and talks. God answered my prayer in month nine, about 290 days into my new lonely life without My Man. My dog, Selah, truly was a turning point for me. Coming home to an empty house wasn't so painful because I had my little red toy poodle for company. I had to take her for walks and train her and spend time with her. Or maybe get a cat. I am allergic to cats, so that was not an option for me. New life around you can help you move forward on your journey.

36th Wedding Anniversary Grief Report, Day 485

I knew something was happening. My body knew. My spirit knew. My mind knew. Deep grief was creeping into my mind. I could not shake it off. It was there with the feeling of not being able to breathe or focus. So much was going through my mind. In four days, Wayman and I would have been celebrating our 36th anniversary on May 19, 2021.

So many questions going through my head — is this an anniversary with Wayman in heaven? Do I still celebrate a marriage when My Man has gone to heaven 485 days before? Questions I still don't have answers to today. But questions I am not afraid to ask God. On this grief journey I have asked hard questions. Sometimes I get answers and sometimes I am left waiting.

The weekend before our anniversary, I could feel a familiar deep grief overwhelm my soul. I was with my family, but I was still so sad. Sunday afternoon and evening, the deep grief felt so familiar. I knew this intense overwhelm well. So, I just went with it. I took a walk. I cried. I remembered.

By Monday evening, it was still deep within my soul. I was missing My Man so intensely. Wishing for a different scenario as I was unloading the dishwasher. Wishing My Man was sitting in his familiar chair in the living room where I could see the back of his head. But he was not. I remember again, our wedding anniversary is approaching in two days. And I cry.

I realized at that moment what a gift it was to be mourning a beautiful holy covenant of marriage. I embraced my grief of losing something so very special and near perfect. This process of grieving is so very complicated with many intricacies and triggers and pain points. But really, so very simple; we grieve for what we no longer have. That which is no longer tangible. I can't reach out and physically touch what I miss.

That night I embraced my deep grief and began thanking God for what I had once embraced but no longer had. Thanksgiving became my prayer of mourning. The love that was deep and wide, high and long from My Man. A marriage worth grieving over. A life lived with the man of my dreams for nearly thirty-five years. Tears came in a flood, but joy was right behind the tears. Thankful. Grateful. Loved. Peaceful.

The next day held more grief. Sweet memories. I went with what was unfolding in my spirit and heart. As Wednesday dawned, I was better. Better in the way that a deep comfort had come into my spirit and found my deep grief. I had planned to spend our anniversary with my children and grandchildren. I had learned to make plans to be with people I love on hard days. I needed support. I needed people.

A friend sent a message to look for surprises from God on this special anniversary day. The surprises were beautiful and were right from God's heart to my heart. A visit to the cemetery was on my list. Of course, I needed to visit the grave of My Man on our anniversary. I love taking flowers from my garden to Wayman's grave. I left my house in a hurry, to get to my workout, without any fresh cut flowers. So? I would buy some in the grocery store. I walked around and looked but nothing felt right. Then I saw the field full of wildflowers right before I turned into the cemetery. Freshly blooming bluebonnets more than a month past their peak — a surprise. The Indian blankets blooming with yellow and brown; standing so tall. A surprise. The same flower he would never cut near our driveway because he wanted to enjoy their blooms on the way to get the mail. A beautiful heart shaped rock a few feet from his grave — a surprise. A few first giggles from my ten-week-old grandson, Ezekiel — a surprise. A huge bouquet of flowers with roses from my son for my anniversary — a surprise. But the greatest surprise was how God took my mourning and turned it to joy as I remembered with thanksgiving, I did have something to grieve. And God was ok with the grieving because He had given me a beautiful, holy covenant relationship with My Man. I could celebrate what I had lost. My grief was transformed into thanksgiving — a surprise.

> "Weeping may last through the night, but joy comes with the morning.
>
> Psalm 30:5 NLT

The Scale of Grief vs. Comfort

Being in deep grief for months on end beyond the first 100 days is a difficult place to continue to live. I was weary of my deep grief, of my bleeding, broken heart because My Man was not by my side anymore. Wave after wave of grief came over me where I could not breathe or seem to move out from under the weight of the crashing waves.

I started asking God for His deep comfort. I reminded God what He had said in Matthew 5:4 NLT "God blesses *those who mourn, for they will be comforted.*" I so wanted this kind of comfort promised by Jesus Himself! In Greek, comfort is "parakaleo," meaning to call to, to exhort, to encourage.

In October 2020, I said to God, "I am in such deep grief. I am asking You to send Your deep comfort to me as You promised in Matthew." Come, Jesus. Come, Holy Spirit. Come into the places of my deep grief in the crevasses of my soul and bring Your Holy Spirit deep comfort. I don't know how to get this comfort from You that will be greater than my grief. But I want Your kind of comfort. A deep holy comfort only from You.

It was a few weeks before the one-year anniversary of Wayman's death and my grief was heavy. I could tell these upcoming weeks would be hard. Maybe even more difficult than the last few months because my body and soul and spirit remember deeply on anniversaries and birthdays and holidays. Tears. Despair. Emptiness. Loneliness. Oh, God, I need You in this season of remembering. The pain. The ambulance. The prayers. The hospital. The machines. The surgery. The sounds in the ICU. The long nights. The long days. The waiting. The visits. The phone calls to the other side of the world. The decisions. The love poured out.

109

The prayers. The waiting. The talks. The songs. The hope. The prayers. The last breath. The wailing. The tears. The prayers. The thanksgiving. The blessings. The crying. The memories. The tears. The visitation. The friends. The family. The celebration of life. The bugle call. The graveside. The love. The thanksgiving. The prayers.

In these few weeks my rhythm of life consisted of getting up and living another day to remember My Man. To find the purposes God had for me. Now. This side of heaven. To not be afraid to express my loneliness. My sadness. My grief. And allowing God to fill my broken heart. Allowing Him to put pressure on the wounds to slow the bleeding. I could feel a shift in my heart. I could breathe easier without gasping for air from the crashing waves of grief.

For the very first time since Wayman passed, I felt the deep comfort of God more than the deep grief of losing Wayman. I saw the scales of justice with the two bowls hanging from the metal bar. One bowl holds my deep grief. One bowl holds God's deep comfort. In my vision, and in my heart, I felt God's comfort weighing more than my grief for the first time since Wayman took his last breath on earth. Wow! This is what it feels like to have the deep comfort of Jesus, I thought.

It was a beautiful revelation and celebration of thanksgiving to God to feel more comfort than sadness. I could only be thankful to God who is sending me His deep comfort through the Holy Spirit. Words cannot give this feeling of holy comfort justice. It is in the spiritual realm.

The call of my heart for God to bring me His deep comfort as promised is still progressing. I can celebrate all that I had with My Man. I am thankful. I am grateful. I am blessed. I am comforted beyond words. Only God can make the bowl of deep comfort overflow.

> *"The Lord is close to the brokenhearted and saves those who are crushed in spirit."*
>
> Psalm 34:18 NIV

The Pit of Despair — The Fight for My Life

June 29, 2021

Psalm 40:1-3 NLT

"I waited patiently for the Lord to help me,
and he turned to me and heard my cry.
He lifted me out of the pit of despair,
out of the mud and the mire.
He set my feet on solid ground
and steadied me as I walked along.
He has given me a new song to sing,
a hymn of praise to our God.
Many will see what he has done and be amazed.
They will put their trust in the Lord."

I have been down this road before. I could feel the familiar darkness and pain. Hopelessness was creeping in on my heart like a thief. The pit was ever so near, a slippery, sliding road leading to deep depression and no purpose. I did not want to write this part of my story to put in my book on grief. But I had to be authentic and vulnerable for you. I believe this part of my story will help you. And help others. And help you help others. See, this experience was beyond my first 100 days of grief.

Somewhere beyond the first 200 days I crashed. I had come to the end of trying to survive this grief. This broken, bleeding heart of mine realizing I would not have My Man by my side again this side of heaven.

I had to let you know the deep wrenching grief continues past the first 100 days. The deep grief that seemed was never ending. The lonely nights. The empty house. The empty table. The empty chair. The empty bed. The empty garden. The empty workshop. The empty heart of mine. There are no secrets in this road of grief. It is lonely. It is hard. The pain was not ending. I couldn't feel the comfort I was promised. I cried out to God. A deep yearning for my life to be different. And I was still alone.

So, for a few days, I crashed. I was ready for heaven. I knew what it was like to live in the darkness of deep depression as I had conquered depression more than ten years ago. Counseling and God helped pull me out of the pit before, and God had steadied me. But here I was, more than 200 days past Wayman's death, knowing I did not want to live. I was finished. But God. On one of my darkest days a friend called to check on me. I told her I was slipping into darkness. She asked if I would talk to a grief counselor. I replied that I would like that. I knew I needed professional help. The next day I had a Zoom appointment and a follow-up session. God met me in my deep grief by the green pastures and still waters of Psalm 23. I actually went to this place of restoration in my mind and met Jesus there. I saw in color as my deep grief and hopelessness were lifted away. He lifted enough of the pain to help me out of the pit of despair. He pulled me out of the mud and mire. He steadied my feet. He said He would always be with me.

I am so very thankful God sent me help quickly in my time of need. I needed help. I got it quickly before I sank too low. I know God sent me help. Would you ask for help if you felt hopeless and finished? God sees you and will lift you out of the pit of despair. This is His promise, and He keeps His promises. Psalm 23 is a treasured song for me. May God bless you with help and answers to your cries in your journey.

Psalm 23:1-3 AMP

"The Lord is my Shepherd [to feed,
to guide and to shield me],

I shall not want.

He lets me lie down in green pastures.

He leads me beside the still and quiet waters.

He refreshes and restores my soul (life).

He leads me in the paths of righteousness

for His name's sake."

What Helped Me When
I Was Grieving

1. Hot baths with Epsom salts

2. Eating dark chocolate

3. Taking several walks a day with a friend, family member, or alone

4. Buying fresh flowers to enjoy

5. Having someone sit with me and let me cry

6. Exercise

7. Prayer

8. Journaling

9. Staying at a family member or friend's house

10. Playing with a puppy

11. Green tea, or any drink that is comforting and warm

12. Family and friends who supported me and were there for me

13. Trust in God's timing

14. Faith!!!

What NOT to Say or Do for Someone Who Is Grieving

"It's going to get better."

We need to sit in our grief. Yes, it will get better. But you do not need to tell them this. They need to be ok right in the middle of their grief and to know that is ok. When you tell them *"It is going to get better,"* it feels like you are trying to take away their grief. They need to sit in it because it *is* a great loss. We need to feel it and be in the middle of the pain. We need to grieve to move through the grief.

"The pain will go away."

Again, just as above, we don't need anyone trying to solve our grief. It is so real. It is so big. Do not diminish their pain by telling them it will go away. We need to feel the pain to get through the pain. I know it is hard to understand this reality. Sometimes I don't understand it either. But our pain equals our love.

"The pain is never going away."

Oh, please do not tell them this. I can't even breathe when I hear this. I know my pain is so great it feels like it will be with me for eternity. But the heaviness of it never leaving is not helpful. And you do not know the unique patterns of grief for each individual. It is a personal and unique journey for each grieving person.

"The second year will be harder than the first year."

How do you know, really? Do you think that statement is going to bring them comfort? Please do not speak words of what your grief did to you onto them and their timeline. Each of us moves through grief uniquely. That is the beauty of grief, not one journey is the same. Let your grief journey be your own.

"Let me tell you about my loss, etc."

I do not have the capacity to comprehend my own loss, much less yours. It is too much for one to attempt to listen to your story. There might be a time and a place to hear your story of loss and grief but wait for the grieving person to ask to hear your story. They are already weighted down, barely keeping their nose above the crashing waves of grief and then you come along to share your story unsolicited. If you are to tell your story, wait. The grieving person will ask you when they are ready. You may need to find a safe person to share and process your grief with as a fresh loss can bring up so much from the past. Find that safe person to process with but please do not "dump" your grief on the recent griever. Be ultra-sensitive and share your own story only when asked.

"Do you think you will remarry?

Seriously, this is not a great question to ask someone who has just lost their spouse. It is not a question anyone wants to answer or even think about at that time. It is not a question that can be answered or should be answered. I was asked this question two different times within the first two weeks of losing Wayman. It did not make me angry or sad, it sort of made me giggle as I could not believe what I was hearing. Like, really?

Grief is the work assignment for survivors.

What TO Say or Do for Someone Who Is Grieving

Talk to them about their loved one. Ask what they miss the most about him/her.

We likely need to process out loud. We want to talk about our person. It is such a treat to be able to freely talk about them. Our loved one's name being said aloud is a balm to the heart. Share memories you have of their loved one and times the person helped you or made you laugh. Of course, there will likely be tears. Let them flow.

"How are you doing today? How are you doing right now?"

This is my number one favorite question of all time. Don't ask if you do not have the time to listen and witness my current state of grief. The emphasis is on "you!" When someone asks me these questions, I can be honest and tell them. They really want to know how I am doing. They are giving me an invitation to tell them the truth of the hard things. And the ok things and the good things. There may not be much good. It can be really hard to talk about how we are actually doing, but it is important to be real and raw. If we are too real and raw, family and friends will worry. And the truth is, one minute you can be doing great in the first thirty seconds of that minute and the last thirty seconds of that same minute may be a crash and burn moment of deep groaning and crying.

It is so important to add in the last part of this question—"today" or "right now." Otherwise, the answers running through our heads are, "You are crazy! How do you think I am doing? I just lost my husband! (Son, wife, daughter, etc.) What a stupid question!

I cannot emphasize enough the importance of this question. Listen. Let them talk. And do not try to take away the tears or pain. You can't.

Just listen with a heart of love and concern. This is called "witnessing grief." It is the number one thing we need — someone to witness our grief. Don't try to fix it, just listen with compassion as they share where they are in their grief journey.

As grief is so very unique to each person, this question may not be appropriate for some. As one mom who buried her young son responded, "How do you think I am doing?" It was not a question that brought her comfort, only more pain. Be aware of each person's unique journey. Be sure to add the important aspect of "current" feelings and emotions with a caring and compassionate intent.

"What is the hardest time of day for you?"

This question can be so helpful for us to process the reality of this question. The answer certainly can fluctuate but it can be useful in knowing how to help the griever. As mentioned previously, one of my out of state friends called me every evening about 9 p.m. for several months. (Thanks so much, Mary Lou. God knew I needed those phone calls.) That time of day was brutal for me. The loneliness crept in big when darkness came. No conversation. No companionship. A meal by myself. All the reality of being a widow was facing me head on. Tears would not stop. I cried myself to sleep. I woke up crying. So, honestly, the answer to this question could be ever changing.

"How can I pray for you?"

Oh, we need prayers. Only the God of all Comfort can really comfort us. I love this question. Many times, I haven't known the answer to this question, but then when asked God whispers to my heart what I need prayers for specifically. God is a God of details. He loves for us to pray for each other.

"Just be there."

Reach out to them if you feel the Holy Spirit prompting you to do so. Listen to what they say. Send a text, even one emoji, make a phone call, or set up a coffee date. Leave a message if they don't answer. They probably will not answer. No words are needed. Nothing is needed but you. Sometimes your words are too much, anyway.

120

Drop by. Leave a note. Leave some cookies. Drop off fresh vegetables from your garden and a cake. (That was a most special gift delivered by my friend Cindy a few months after Wayman passed. I felt so loved and not forgotten.)

Offer to pick up groceries or do laundry. Stop by with their favorite coffee drink and tissues. Offer to walk the dog or fold laundry. Let them cry and/or sleep while you sit quietly and read or fold laundry. Wrap your arms around them and hold them. Human touch is something they will need desperately at this time.

Set reminders on your calendar for regularly scheduled connections with those grieving.

And once again…Just listen. Do not share your own grief story. Let us talk. Just listen. You can't fix us, so don't even try.

"Show up."

In the first few weeks, we have no idea what we need. We are in shock and just trying to make it through the next fifteen minutes. Drop by and bring a fruit salad or a plate of cookies. Ask if you can clean the bathrooms and vacuum the floors or do the laundry.

"Let us cry."

I have found tears to be one of the most beautiful aspects of my grief journey. I never knew one could cry so much. I truly believe I have cried gallons of tears. There is so much scientific data to show our tears of sorrow look different than our tears of joy or even tears from cutting onions. God created us to release toxins from our tear ducts as we grieve. I feel calmer, more relaxed and grounded almost every time I cry. It is a holy experience. God tells us He is collecting our tears. Well, if He is collecting them, Jesus has to be right there with us, face to face, to collect our tears. Let us cry. I cannot overemphasize this point. Please, let us cry. We need to. We have something to cry about. We are broken-hearted.

> *Heaven is not a threat to me.*

Writing Exercises to Help You Through Your Grief Journey

May I suggest that as you write you sit in the chair or the space your loved one once sat in. Expect the tears to flow. These guidelines gave me some simple structure in my writing which at times was so needed in the midst of my deep grief.

Three Guided Writing Prompts:

1. Write three sentences in any order about any aspect of your grief:

   - A simple observation of something present (My tears taste like salt.)

   - An imperative (giving a command) (Sara, get up and go for a walk.)

   - A sentence that starts with "I" or "you" (I feel like I cannot keep going without you.)

Then, see if they can be rearranged, trimmed, or expanded.

Examples:

   - A tear ran down my cheek.

   - You came to visit me just as I thought I had turned the corner.

   - Keep grieving – there are still memories to relive as love notes.

Keep the legacy alive with photos, conversations, and dreams. Enjoy every single memory of your loved one.

Winter, spring, summer, and fall, each are brimful to running over with special memories.

2. Your topic is your grief. Choose a simple phrase as a refrain and work it into three sentences. Again, notice what happens, opens up, and offers further direction.

Examples:

🕊 Going home is as beautiful as the beginning, and as good.

🕊 We won't be going home until the call of the Father has been heard.

🕊 But every step of the journey, we are actually going home.

Grief produces such a variety of feelings. Sadness, anger, and numbness are some of what grief produces. Grief also produces memories, tears, fears, peace, acceptance, meaning, and love.

3. These are some of my favorite things to ask God in the midst of the creative process and grief. They are powerful! May God unveil more of His purposes for your grief to you in this process of asking questions.

Questions to help you reframe in order to see God's perspective of grief:

🕊 What's happening here? What's God saying?

🕊 What's this about?

🕊 Why is this coming up right now?

🕊 What's emerging?

🕊 What do I notice? What do I notice that I notice?

🕊 What do I/you mean?

🕊 What's outside the frame?

🕊 Where's the invitation?

🕊 Where is your grief? Can you identify where your grief is in your body?

🕊 How would you describe your grief?

🕊 What size is your grief?

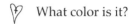 What color is it?

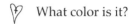 What do you want to say to your grief?

 Can you find a safe place to process your grief?

Note: Writing prompts were adapted from Marilyn McIntyre's online workshop on grief and writing, 2020.

A Letter to My Man

Dear Wayman Lee,

Firsts are so hard. We were one. You passed away. And then I was alone.

The first haircut. You were not there to tell me how you liked it. You always complimented me. By the way, I got a really short haircut. I called it my "lament haircut." I am not sure you would have liked it. But you would have said, "It will grow? Maybe?" You were not one for really short hair on me.

The first workout without you. We always went together to exercise at the gym. You had your trainer and I had mine. We shared this time together. After you were gone, I kept the same routine. I knew I needed to find a rhythm in my exercise routines. I found it easy to cry and sweat at the same time. Liquid pouring from my body in multiple ways. I am so thankful we started that routine about a year before you left. I am still at it twice a week. Now three times a week. You would be impressed by my strength. My trainer brags on me since you are not here to tell me. You know how much I loved encouragement.

The first time to church without you. I cried and cried and cried through it all. I was thankful Jordan was right there beside me. Worshiping God makes everything better.

The first night alone. No one was in the house. You were gone. The dogs were gone. (Justin took them at my request. It was too hard for me to care for them.) I was thankful God had sent angels stationed in and around my home. It is still a place of peace. People can feel it when they walk in. You helped establish our home as a place of peace. Thank you, My Man.

The first time to the bank. I cried. The tellers missed you. The manager cried with me. They remembered your kindness and joy.

The first evening alone. Oh, I dreaded the evening without you. You were my companion. My anchor. We ended our day together in the same room. My tears flowed and sometimes I ended up on the floor groaning and crying with such a deep emptiness. I am so thankful for our many pleasant and happy evenings of companionship we shared.

The time I had to close out your savings account at the credit union. I couldn't stop crying. The final things are so hard. And by the way, I just moved your money over into my account.

The first time I took our walk alone. I cried. I could barely breathe. I just wanted to lay down on the road and kick and scream. Where were you? I miss you so much on my walks. I talk to God. But those 27,000 miles together changed us both for the better. I will still be walking. Less than we did, but I try to get out every day. And now I have a new puppy, Selah, and she ensures I get at least one walk in a day. You would love her so much. She is the absolute cutest puppy on earth.

The first trash day. You always served our family by taking out the trash. Every time it needed to be taken out. And then on trash day, you took the cans to the street. Every Tuesday. I cried and cried when you were not here to do it. Now, I do it the night before. It makes it easier for me. Less tears. Thanks for serving our family all those years. Never complaining. You just took out the trash. Now I do.

The grocery store trips. I cry. I wonder if I am spending too much for fresh raspberries. And large avocados. You always bought the small size. You bought way more groceries than I ever did. You liked buying groceries. I did not like it so much. Plus, I know you thought we saved a bunch of money without me at the store every week. You got the essentials. Thanks for serving me and our boys all these years.

Prepare the garden for planting. Oh, I missed our conversations about what to plant and which bed to plant the tomatoes and peppers in. I cried when I pulled up the last of the fall garden you had planted in late 2019. I hated to pull up those plants, knowing you weren't going to help me anymore. The last reminder of your sowing. And I miss you because some of the raised beds need to be hammered together again. You are not here. I have to ask someone to come help me.

When I come home after being away for a few days. It is so hard to come into an empty, lonely house. Silence greets me like a cold winter storm. Will it ever get better? These transitions are so very painful.

Unloading the car and loading the car for a trip. I load every bag. You are not here to help organize and put everything in its place. And then I dread unloading every item. It is just me. I have to do the unloading. It makes my heart so thankful for how very helpful you were, always working together on simple tasks.

The first season change from winter to spring. I did not want winter to end because that was when you left me. I wanted to remember and remain in that time and season. I am writing this book now after an entire year has passed. Each season passing is difficult. I cried when the air got cooler, and fall was on its way in. You loved each season, but fall was special. I think because hunting season was just a few weeks away.

Holidays and special days without you are awful. I dread them. They are not the same. Birthdays. Easter. Memorial Day. Fourth of July. Just plain awful. I would rather not have any holidays anymore. It would be easier on my heart.

Each new thing without you is like stretching a muscle that has not been moved in years. It is painful and scary, and honestly, sometimes I would just like to stop and jump off this train of life. I have to learn to breathe again. Take a baby step. Maybe fall down but ask for help to get back up. If I cannot do it myself.

And checking the box that says "Widow" instead of "Married" is harder than I could have imagined. It is something I never thought about as being hard. Checking a box. But it is. Without you.

Oh, and when I see your signature, I start crying. I love your signature. It is you. Regal and official and perfect and precise; predictable and flowed with years of practice.

I miss you gently reminding me to push the "cancel" button on the dishwasher after I unload it. The way you knew if the dishes were clean or dirty, instead of having to inspect and guess. Even after thirty-four years, I still forgot to push the "cancel" button when you were here. I wish you were still here to tell me. Actually, I smile every time I do it now. I actually think I am at nearly 100% accuracy, now that you are gone. You would be proud of me.

The first trip without you on an airplane. It has taken more than a year for me to be brave enough. But I am ready again. I couldn't even think of it for weeks. I did not want to go anywhere without you. But now, as I am writing this book, I have three trips planned and booked this year. With more to come. But that first one was so hard.

And I miss using your pen. You always had one in your pocket. Ready and waiting. Now I have to dig in my purse and hope I can find one in the dark abyss that works. It is one of the many, many little things I miss, Wayman Lee Thurman.

I think the list will never end. I keep adding more each time I sit down to write. The list may end up being a million little things and big things I miss about you. Did you know it would be like this? I think you did know. This is what love does when two become one.

I love you still; I will love you forever,

Sara Lee

I love you still; I will love you forever.

A Letter to My Readers Grieving the Loss of a Loved One

If you are reading this book, I assume you are grieving. Oh, Dear One, I am so very sorry you are walking this road of grief. Here I am, continuing to write this book on the first 100-day anniversary of My Man's death. So, 365 plus another 100 days without him. It has been 465 days and counting. I have made it this far. And thanks be to God for giving me breath for more days.

I pray to the God of all comfort to send His deep comfort your way. It may seem like comfort will never come. Or it comes and somehow evaporates so quickly you can't remember how comfort feels, tastes, sounds, looks or smells.

It is a journey no one can experience exactly like you. Your grief journey is unique to you. Embrace your grief. To be grieving so much means you have loved so well. And, by the way, you cannot grieve in wrong ways. May you embrace this journey and feel the feelings of pain and grief. Don't push it away or think you do not have time for grief. Grief is the work assignment for survivors. Embrace your grief head on - the snotty noses, tears falling through the night (into your ears) and into the day (into your shirt.) Grief is the task at hand that has no manual. Except, just take another breath. And another one. May you feel the strength of God and those around you to carry you through to the next minute, the next day. The next month seems too long. This day seems long. So just take your time. You get to make the rules.

Minute by minute embrace your beautiful journey of grief. Deep love results in deep grief. It is a result of a beautiful love. So, grieve, dear one. God is collecting your tears along this journey of grief. I bless you with peace and wish you little snippets of joy to emerge along the pathway. You can do hard things. One minute at a time. One day at a time.

Much love and many blessings,

Sara Thurman

My Anchor Scriptures/Bible Verses Reference Index

Oh, My Lord God. Without these verses to calm my heart and soothe my soul and collect my tears, I could not have made it through the first one hundred days and beyond on my grief journey. Thank You, God, for Your promises and hope infused into these Words of Life. May these Holy Living Words be the breath of life for those who also are on a journey of grief.

Genesis 26:12 NLT

"When Isaac planted his crops that year, he harvested a hundred times more than he planted, for the LORD blessed him."

II Samuel 22:33 NIV

It is God who arms me with strength and keeps my way secure."

II Chronicles 20:21-22 NLT

"After consulting the people, the king appointed singers to walk ahead of the army, singing to the LORD and praising him for his holy splendor. This is what they sang: 'Give thanks to the LORD; His faithful love endures forever!' At the very moment they began to sing and give praise, the Lord caused the armies of Ammon, Moab, and Mount Seir to start fighting among themselves."

Nehemiah 8:10 NLT

"...the joy of the Lord is your strength."

Psalms 1:3 TPT

"He will be standing firm like a flourishing tree planted by God's design, deeply rooted by the brook of bliss, bearing fruit in every season of life. He is never dry, never fainting, ever blessed, ever prosperous."

Psalm 3:8 TPT

"For the Lord alone is my Savior. What a feast of favor and bliss He gives His people."

Psalms 9:10 NLT

"Those who know your name trust in you, for you, O Lord, will not abandon those who search for you."

Psalm 18:19 NLT

"He led me to a place of safety; He rescued me because He delights in me."

Psalm 18:19-24 TPT

"His love broke open the way, and he brought me into a beautiful, broad place. He rescued me — because his delight is in me! He rewarded me for doing what's right and staying pure. I will follow his commands and I'll not sin by ceasing to follow him, no matter what. For I've kept my eyes focused on his righteous words, and I've obeyed everything that he's told me to do. I've been blameless before him and followed all his ways, keeping my heart pure. And so, Yahweh has rewarded me according to my righteousness, because I kept my heart clean before his eyes."

Psalms 23:1-3 The Amplified Version

"The Lord is my Shepherd [to feed, to guide and to shield me], I shall not want. He lets me lie down in green pastures; He leads me beside the still and quiet waters. He refreshes and restores my soul (life); He leads me in the paths of righteousness for His name's sake."

Psalm 23:4 TPT

"Even when your path takes me through the valley of deepest darkness, fear will never conquer me, for You already have! Your authority is my strength and my peace. The comfort of Your love takes away my fear. I'll never be lonely, for you are near."

Psalms 23:4 NLT

"Even when I walk through the darkest valley, I will not be afraid, for you are close beside me. Your rod and your staff protect and comfort me."

Psalm 27:14 TPT

"Here's what I've learned through it all: Don't give up; don't be impatient; be entwined as one with the Lord. Be brave and courageous, and never lose hope. Yes, keep on waiting — for He will never disappoint you!"

Psalm 30:5 NLT

"Weeping may last through the night, but joy comes with the morning."

Psalm 34:5 TPT

"Gaze upon Him, join your life with His, and joy will come. Your faces will glisten with glory. You'll never wear that shame-face again."

Psalms 34:18 TPT

"The Lord is close to all whose hearts are crushed by pain."

Psalm 34:18 NIV

"The Lord is close to the brokenhearted and saves those who are crushed in spirit."

Psalm 40:1-3 NLT

"I waited patiently for the Lord to help me, and he turned to me and heard my cry. He lifted me out of the pit of despair, out of the mud and the mire. He set my feet on solid ground and steadied me as I walked along. He has given me a new song to sing, a hymn of praise to our God. Many will see what he has done and be amazed. They will put their trust in the Lord."

Psalms 46:4 NLT

"A river brings joy to the city of our God."

Psalm 56:8 NLT

"You keep track of all of my sorrows. You have collected all my tears in Your bottle. You have recorded each one in Your book."

Psalm 65:11 NLT

"You crown the year with a bountiful harvest; even the hard pathways overflow with abundance."

Psalms 67:1 TPT

"God, keep us near your mercy-fountain and bless us! And when you look down on us, may your face beam with joy!" Pause in His presence (Selah)

Psalms 69:3, 29, 32 NLT

"I am exhausted from crying for help; my throat is parched. My eyes are swollen with weeping, waiting for my God to help me. I am suffering and in pain. Rescue me, O God, by your saving power. The humble will see their God at work and be glad. Let all who seek God's help be encouraged."

Psalms 72:17 TPT

"So that His name may be honored forever! May the fame of His name spring forth! May it shine on, like the sunshine! In Him all will be blessed to bless others and may all the people bless the One who blessed them."

Psalms 89:5 NLT

"All heaven will praise Your great wonders, Lord; myriads of angels will praise You for Your faithfulness."

Psalm 89:15, 17 NLT

"Happy are those who hear the joyful call to worship, for they will walk in the light of Your presence, Lord. You are their glorious strength. It pleases You to make us strong."

Psalms 91:1 TPT

"When you abide under the shadow of Shaddai (God of the Mountain, God the Destroyer of Enemies, God the Self-Sufficient One, God the Nurturer of Babies, God the Almighty), you are hidden in the strength of God Most High."

Psalms 91:9-10a TPT

"When we live our lives within the shadow of God Most High, our secret hiding place, we will always be shielded from harm."

Psalms 111:2 NLT

"How amazing are the deeds of the Lord! All who delight in Him should ponder them."

Psalms 121:1-2 NLT

"I look up to the mountains—does my help come from there? My help comes from the Lord, who made heaven and earth!"

Psalms 121:3-4 TPT

"He will guard and guide me, never letting me stumble or fall. God is my keeper; He will never forget nor ignore me. He will never slumber or sleep; He is the Guardian-God for His people, Israel."

Psalms 139:1-2 TPT

"Lord, You know everything there is to know about me. You perceive every movement of my heart and soul, and You understand my every thought before it even enters my mind."

Psalms 139:4-5 NLT

"You know what I am going to say even before I say it, Lord. You go before me and follow me. You place Your hand of blessing on my head."

Psalms 139:16 TPT

"You saw who You created me to be before I became me! Before I'd ever seen the light of day, the number of days You plans for me were already recorded in Your book."

Proverbs 3:6 NLT

"Seek His will in all you do, and He will show you which path to take."

Proverbs 31:13-14 TPT

"She searches out continually to possess that which is pure and righteous. She delights in the work of her hands. She gives out revelation-truth to feed others. She is like a trading ship bringing divine supplies from the merchant."

Song of Songs 2:10 NLT

"My lover said to me, 'Rise up my darling! Come away with Me, My fair one!'"

Song of Songs 2:10 TPT

"The one I love calls to Me: Arise, My dearest. Hurry, My darling. Come away with Me! I have come as you have asked to draw you to My heart and lead you out. For now, is the time, My beautiful one."

Isaiah 1:19 TPT

"If you have a willing heart to let Me help you, and if you will obey Me, you will feast on the blessings of an abundant harvest."

Isaiah 26:2-3 NLT

"Open the gates to all who are righteous; allow the faithful to enter. You will keep in perfect peace all who trust in You, all whose thoughts are fixed on You!"

Isaiah 28:12 TPT

"This is your rest, so let the weary rest; this is your comfort..."

Isaiah 41:10 NLT

"Don't be afraid, for I am with you. Don't be discouraged, for I am your God. I will strengthen you and help you. I will hold you up with my victorious right hand."

Isaiah 51:12 NLT

"I, yes I, am the One who comforts you."

Isaiah 55:8-9 NLT

"My thoughts are nothing like your thoughts," says the LORD. "And My ways are far beyond anything you could imagine. For just as the heavens are higher than the earth, so My ways are higher than your ways and My thoughts higher than your thoughts."

Isaiah 55:11-13 NLT

"It is the same with my word. I send it out, and it always produces fruit. It will accomplish all I want it to, and it will prosper everywhere I send it. You will live in joy and peace. The mountains and hills will burst into song, and the trees of the field will clap their hands! Where once there were thorns, cypress trees will grow. Where nettles grew, myrtles will

sprout up. These events will bring great honor to the Lord's name; they will be an everlasting sign of His power and love."

Isaiah 58:8-9 NLT

"Then your salvation will come like the dawn, and your wounds will quickly heal. Your godliness will lead you forward, and the glory of the Lord will protect you from behind. Then, when you call, the Lord will answer. 'Yes, I am here,' He will quickly reply..."

Isaiah 66:18 TPT

"The time is coming for Me to gather people together from all over the world, and they will come and gaze on My radiance."

Jeremiah 31:3 NLT

"I have loved you, My people, with an everlasting love. With an unfailing love I have drawn you to Myself."

Jeremiah 31:6 NLT

"Come, let us go up to Jerusalem to worship the Lord our God."

Jeremiah 31: 9 NLT

"Tears of joy will stream down their faces, and I will lead them home with great care. They will walk beside quiet streams and on smooth paths where they will not stumble."

Jeremiah 31:13b NLT

"I will turn their mourning into joy. I will comfort them and exchange their sorrow for rejoicing."

Jeremiah 33:3 NLT

"Ask me and I will tell you remarkable secrets you do not know about things to come."

Ezekiel 47:5-7 NLT

"Then he measured another 1,750 feet, and the river was too deep to walk across. It was deep enough to swim in, but too deep to walk through. He asked me, "Have you been watching, son of man?" Then he led me back along the riverbank. When I returned, I was surprised by the sight of many trees growing on both sides of the river."

Ezekiel 47:9 NLT

"...life will flourish wherever this river flows."

Amos 9:10 NLT

"On that day I will restore the fallen house of David. I will repair its damaged walls. From the ruins I will rebuild it and restore its former glory."

Habakkuk 2:4b NLT

"But the righteousness will live by their faithfulness to God."

Habakkuk 2:14 NLT

"For as the waters fill the sea, the earth will be filled with an awareness of the glory of the Lord."

Habakkuk 3:17-19 NLT

"Even though the fig trees have no blossoms, and there are no grapes on the vines; even though the olive crop fails, and the fields lie empty and barren; even though the flocks die in the fields, and the cattle barns are empty, yet I will rejoice in the Lord! I will be joyful in the God of my salvation! The Sovereign Lord is my strength! He makes me as surefooted as a deer, able to tread upon the heights."

Haggai 2:4-5 NLT

"'Be strong...Be strong, all you people still left in the land. And now get to work, for I am with you,' says the Lord of Heaven's

Armies. My Spirit remains among you, just as I promised...So do not be afraid."'

Haggai 2:6-9, 19 NLT

"For this is what the Lord of Heaven's Armies says: In just a little while I will again shake the heavens and the earth, the oceans and the dry land. I will shake all the nations, and the treasures of all the nations will be brought to this Temple. I will fill this place with glory, says the Lord of Heaven's Armies. The silver is mine, and the gold is mine, says the Lord of Heaven's Armies. The future glory of this Temple will be greater than its past glory, says the Lord of Heaven's Armies. And in this place, I will bring peace. I, the Lord of Heaven's Armies, have spoken!"

Matthew 5:4 NLT

"God blesses those who mourn, for they will be comforted."

Matthew 7:13 TPT

"The narrow gate and the difficult way leads to eternal life—so few even find it!"

Matthew 11:28 TPT

"Are you weary, carrying a heavy burden? Come to Me. I will refresh your life, for I am your oasis."

Matthew 14:29 TPT

" 'Come and join me,' Jesus replied. So, Peter stepped out onto the water and began to walk toward Jesus."

John 12:35-36 NLT

"Jesus replied, 'My light will shine for you just a little longer. Walk in the light while you can, so the darkness will not overtake you. Those who walk in the darkness cannot see

where they are going. Put your trust in the light while there is still time; then you will become children of light.'"

John 15:5 NLT

"Yes, I am the vine; you are the branches. Those who remain in Me, and I in them, will produce much fruit. For apart from Me you can do nothing."

Acts 20:24 NLT

"But my life is worth nothing to me unless I use it for finishing the work assigned to me by the Lord Jesus — the work of telling others the Good News about the wonderful grace of God."

Romans 8:38 NLT

"And I am convinced that nothing can ever separate us from God's love. Neither death nor life, neither angels nor demons, neither our fears for today nor our worries about tomorrow — not even the powers of hell can separate us from God's love."

Romans 15:13 NLT

"I pray that God, the source of hope, will fill you completely with joy and peace because you trust in Him. Then you will overflow with confident hope through the power of the Holy Spirit."

2 Corinthians 4:18 TPT

"… because we don't focus our attention on what is seen but on what is unseen. For what is seen is temporary, but the unseen realm is eternal."

Galatians 1:10-11 NLT

"Obviously, I'm not trying to win the approval of people, but of God. If pleasing people was my goal, I would not be Christ's servant."

Philippians 1:6 NLT

"And I am certain that God, who began the good work within you, will continue His work until it is finally finished on the day when Christ Jesus returns."

Colossians 3:17 TPT

"Let every activity of your lives and every word that comes from your lips be drenched with the beauty of our Lord Jesus, the Anointed One. And bring your constant praise to God the Father because of what Christ has done for you!"

I Timothy 1:5 NLT

"The purpose of my instruction is that all believers would be filled with love that comes from a pure heart, a clear conscience, and genuine faith."

I Timothy 6:17, 21 TPT

"To all the rich of this world, I command you not to be wrapped in thoughts of pride over your prosperity, or rely on your wealth, for your riches are unreliable and nothing compared to the living God. Trust instead in the one who lavishes upon us all good things, fulfilling our every need .... May God's grace empower you always!""

Hebrews 12:2 TPT

"We look away from the natural realm and we focus our attention and expectation onto Jesus who birthed faith within us and who leads us forward into faith's perfection. His example is this: Because His heart was focused on the joy of knowing that you would be His, He endured the agony of the cross and conquered its humiliation, and now sits exalted at the right hand of the throne of God!"

Hebrews 12:2 NLT

"Keeping our eyes on Jesus, the pioneer and perfecter of our faith. For the joy that lay before Him, He endured the cross, despising the shame."

James 5:13-17 NLT

"Are any of you suffering hardships? You should pray. Are any of you happy? You should sing praises. Are any of you sick? You should call for the elders of the church to come and pray over you, anointing you with oil in the name of the Lord. Such a prayer offered in faith will heal the sick, and the Lord will make you well. And if you have committed any sins, you will be forgiven. Confess your sins to each other and pray for each other so that you may be healed. The earnest prayer of a righteous person has great power and produces wonderful results."

I Peter 5:7 NLT

"Give all your worries and cares to God, for he cares about you."

I Peter 5:7 TPT

"Pour out all your worries and stress upon Him and leave them there, for He always tenderly cares for you."

Jude 1b-2 NLT

"I am writing to all who have been called by God the Father, who loves you and keeps you safe in the care of Jesus Christ. May God give you more and more mercy, peace, and love."

Revelation 5:10-11 NLT

"And you have caused them to become a Kingdom of priests for our God. And they will reign on the earth. Then I looked again, and I heard the voices of thousands and millions of angels around the throne and of the living beings and the elders."

Revelation 5:11-12 TPT

"Then I looked, and I heard the voices of myriads of angels in circles around the throne, as well as the voices of the living creatures and the elders — myriads and myriads! And as I watched, all of them were singing with thunderous voices: 'Worthy is Christ the Lamb who was slaughtered to receive great power and might, wealth and wisdom, and honor, glory, and praise!'"

Revelation 7:12 NLT

"They sang, 'Amen! Blessing and glory and wisdom and thanksgiving and honor and power and strength belong to our God forever and ever! Amen.'"

Acknowledgements

Acknowledgements to the family and friends who came along beside me during those pain filled first 100 Days and beyond:

Jordan, Evangeline, and Hepzibah, Justin, Ana, and Lilian, Jared, Donna, and Jonah, Julie and Murray, Ann, Judy, Mary Lou, Mary, Cecilia, Donna and Steve, Julie, Peggy, Christy and Jake, Paula, Genavieve, Honee, Alan and Shara, Jose, Tammie and Mark, Jenni and Matt, and the list continues. Thank you! Your love sustained me in my darkest days and nights. You helped me know there was a light burning somewhere when I could not see even a glimmer of it. Thank you. I am so grateful for your love and care and kindness in acknowledging my grief and not being afraid of witnessing my pain. I pray I can now be a help to others in their grief journey.

I am so thankful for Kristen, Maira, and Kristin for helping me make this book a reality. God set up holy intersections with each of you to assist me in getting my story of grief to a place of excellence and released to the world. Your ever-present guidance, tenderness, and love helped me tell my story about My Man and that is a true gift to my heart and soul.

My Cup

By Sara Thurman

The rain mends my broken heart, one healing drop at a time in my cup

Come pour on my container of life a gentle and welcoming holy oil

Your timing breathed healing hope into my cup of grief

Resources

These additional books by Sara Thurman, EdD are available on Amazon.

Small Beginnings: A Journey to the Impossible

A memoir of how Sara became an artist at age fifty-six with no previous art background. Written with ten steps, unfolding in her own small beginnings story.

Small Beginnings Companion Prayer Journal: A Journey to the Impossible

A companion prayer journal to enhance your story of small beginnings, following the ten steps from Sara's memoir.

How Good Can God Be? A Story About a Little Girl and Her Daddy

Sara's first children's book, written about her earthly father being a prototype of our Heavenly Father's love. Written and illustrated by Sara.

Companion Reflection Journal, Reflecting on Grief and Moving Beyond Pain

A personal journal for the reader to reflect with their own writings as they move through the first 100 days of their grief story.

Below items are only available at sarathurman.com

Scripture Affirmations Cards for Grief with Original Art: Card Set 1

And

Scripture Affirmations Cards for Grief with Original Art: Card Set 2

These scripture cards are taken from Sara's first 100 days of grief using helpful scriptures from the Bible in those first days. They are printed on some of her original artwork to inspire you. Sara's prayer is that these cards may bring hope and peace to you on a daily basis as you journey through your own loss.

Additional card sets will become available on Sara's website in the future.

About The Author

Sara Thurman, EdD is founder of **Acts 1:8 Blessings**, a creative art ministry serving creatives all over the world. Sara facilitates spiritual creative retreats, mentors, teaches, writes, and paints to share her love of the connections with God in this devotional process. Sara is also the host of a podcast *Small Beginnings with Sara.* After a successful Season 1 with 25 episodes in which guests presented their own Small Beginnings, she is now working on Season 2, which will also include people's grief stories and how they have walked through grief as their small beginnings. Her authenticity in sharing her own experience draws others to share their story through creativity.

Sara has written two #1 bestselling books, *Small Beginnings: A Journey to the Impossible*, her memoir of becoming a prominent artist in her late 50's with no previous art experience, encouraging others to take the first steps for their own small beginnings, along with an accompanying journal. In 2021, she wrote and illustrated her first children's book, *How Good Can God Be?*, using her own childhood memories of God's goodness on a Texas ranch. Her most recent book, *Reflecting on Grief and Moving Beyond Pain: Living with Loss and Discovering New Meaning,* presents journal entries and reflections on living with loss and discovering new meaning within the first 100 days after her husband passed from this earthly life into eternity.

Sara enjoys life in Wimberley, Texas when she is not on an adventure traveling the world inspiring others on their journey of creativity. Sara lives to motivate and tell others all over the world about the goodness of God through creativity all.

Made in the USA
Coppell, TX
29 November 2021

66706521R00095